The Hermeneutics of an African-Igbo Theology

Peter Chidi Okuma

The Hermeneutics of an African-Igbo Theology

Bibliographic Information published by the Deutsche Nationalbibliothek
The Deutsche Nationalbibliothek lists this publication in the Deutsche Nationalbibliografie; detailed bibliographic data is available in the internet at http://dnb.d-nb.de.

Library of Congress Cataloging-in-Publication Data
Okuma, Peter Chidi.
The hermeneutics of an African-Igbo theology / Peter Chidi Okuma.
pages cm
Includes bibliographical references.
ISBN 978-3-631-66455-1
1. Christianity—Nigeria. 2. Igbo (African people)—Religion. 3. Theology, Practical—Nigeria. I. Title.
BR1463.N5O378 2015
276.69008996332—dc23

2015017895

ISBN 978-3-631-66455-1 (Print)
E-ISBN 978-3-653-05636-5 (E-Book)
DOI 10.3726/978-3-653-05636-5

© Peter Lang GmbH
Internationaler Verlag der Wissenschaften
Frankfurt am Main 2015
All rights reserved.
Peter Lang Edition is an Imprint of Peter Lang GmbH.

Peter Lang – Frankfurt am Main · Bern · Bruxelles · New York · Oxford · Warszawa · Wien

All parts of this publication are protected by copyright. Any utilisation outside the strict limits of the copyright law, without the permission of the publisher, is forbidden and liable to prosecution. This applies in particular to reproductions, translations, microfilming, and storage and processing in electronic retrieval systems.

This publication has been peer reviewed.

www.peterlang.com

Preface

Reading this book is, for a European theologian like me, an enriching experience. It not only challenges my thinking from the perspective of African values and especially the Igbo tradition, it also reinforces an insight which I share with contemporary innovative theologians such as Stanley Hauerwas: theology, like every attempt to understand reality and to articulate its symbolic reference to transcendence, starts with a new way of looking at the world. It reminds me of the words of Barbara Ward quoted in the report of the UN Commission on World Governance ("Our Common Neighbourhood"): *"The most important change that people can make is to change their way of looking at the world. We can change studies, jobs, neighbourhoods, even countries and continents and still remain much as we always were. But change our fundamental angle of vision and everything changes -our priorities, our values, our judgments, our pursuits. Again and again, in the history of religion, this total upheaval in the imagination has marked the beginning of a new life... a turning of the heart, a 'metanoia' by which men see with new eyes and understand with new minds and turn their energies to new ways of living"*[1].

With this book Peter Okuma introduces the reader into an hermeneutical theology, which takes distance from the rational presuppositions that have been dominating academic theology in the northern hemisphere for centuries, especially since modernity with its rationality connected with individualistic bourgeois interests and the instrumentalization of life.

Peter Okuma's starting point is recognition of the socio-linguistic structuration of experience. Our experience of the world as meaningful is not evident in itself, nor is it based on merely rational knowledge. It is also and basically qualified by our adherence to a living and narrative framework of interpretation: as Christians, we experience the world as meaningful from the perspective of the biblical metanarrative, which interrupts hermeneutic perspectives dominated by the influential but often hidden story of the

---

1 Barbara Ward as quoted in *Our Global Neighbourhood. The Report of the Commission on Global Governance*, Oxford, Oxford University Press, 1995, p. 47.

economic and technological globalization of the world. It opens our eyes again for the hidden dimensions of reality and for new meanings, which enrich our experience of being human. Because the gospel gives us access to a horizon of interpretation which is different from that of modernity and its types of rationality, we can generate and incarnate new and more human ways of being and acting, and liberate ourselves from the illusions of a world dominated by economic success and individualism.

For Peter Okuma this hermeneutic turn is not an abstract event. It is inserted in real life, in the church experience of Igbo women and men whose life is rooted in a Eucharistic encounter with Christ. This encounter shapes a community, which bears witness of new life in an old world.

Prof. Dr. Johan Verstraeten
Faculty of Theology
Catholic University of Leuven, Belgium.

Dedication

- In loving Memory of my beloved Papa Richard, and my Cherished Mother, Chiamaka
- In loving memory of my friend and Classmate, Rev. Fr Thomas Ezechukwu

And

- In passionate memory of Opa Josef Dötzer

"The Ibo is at heart a child, with all a child's winsomeness. He loves fun and banter. If you show him the good side of your character, he will show you the best side of his. Any missionary who does not succeed in winning the good-will of nearly all the people is himself at fault. Their judgment of us is generally correct, and they know a good man when they meet one. Their souls aspire to goodness; they have not stifled the aspiration. It is my firm conviction that we shall meet great numbers of our Ibos, pagans as well as practically all our Catholics, in heaven."

- John P. Jordan, (c.s.s.p.), *Bishop Shanahan of Southern Nigeria*, Dublin, 1949, p. 122.

Table Of Contents

Introduction 13

Chapter One: The Narrative Behind the Hermeneutics 19

Chapter Two: The Story of All Stories:
The Resurrection of Christ! 29

Chapter Three: The Igbo Worldview at the
Service of a Theology 43

Chapter Four: The Paradox of a Spirituality 63

Chapter Five: A Theology at the Service of the People:
Igbo Situations and the World Order 81

Chapter Six: Conclusion 101

Bibliography 107

About The Book 117

Other Books by Peter Chidi Okuma published
by Peter Lang Academic Publishers 119

Introduction

It is arguably true that one of the seemingly most balanced and erudite works written on the evangelization of the Igbo (Ibo) vis-à-vis their *Sitz-im-leben* (living situation) is the 1949 work of John J. Jordan (c.s.s.p) titled: *Bishop Shanahan of Southern Nigeria*. One of the reasons for this seemingly successful effort was the firsthand and apparent balanced account of the author (who was Educational Adviser to the Catholic Missions of Nigeria and the British Cameroons)[2] within the world of the Igbo that he saw. This is *au courant* with the argument of Stanley Hauerwas that "we can only act within the world we can see and we can see the world rightly by being trained to see. We do not come to see just by looking, but by disciplined skills developed through initiation into a narrative. We cannot see the world rightly unless we are changed, because contrary to our assumptions, we do not desire to see the world truthfully."[3] The life of a people, the narrative of a people – their story, their worldview is a way of 'seeing' a people, of being initiated into the people and consequently being able to see them truly.[4]

This 'way of initiation' could be called in our context here a hermeneutics. Where this has to do with the 'biblical metanarrative' as we attempted here, it becomes "a very complex activity with receptive and creative dimensions."[5] In this way, this technical term, hermeneutics here denotes this activity of "encountering" that brings the biblical metanarrative in *pari-pasu* with the story of a people, their worldview, their *Sitz im Leben* into perspective. This is so as much as we take cognizance of the truism that, "Faith is based on such encounters. It is a human activity: there is no way to speak about the transcendent or about God outside of its or God's relation to the world or to human life. If one wants to speak about the transcendence, if one wants to speak about God, one cannot but

---

2 Cf. J. P. Jordan, (c.s.s.p.), *Bishop Shanahan of Southern Nigeria*, Dublin, 1949.
3 S. Hauerwas, *The Peaceable Kingdom: A Primer in Christian Ethics,* Notre Dame, 1983, p. 29.
4 See, C. Achebe, *Things Fall Apart,* London, Ibadan, Nairobi, 1969.
5 J. Haers, "A Risk Observed" in *Louvain Studies* 21(1996), p. 47.

speak about the universe and about human experiences... Interestingly, in the Christian tradition, this appreciation of transcendence is enshrined in the incarnation, in the life of Jesus Christ, where Christians discover both God's face oriented towards human beings and the world, and a human face oriented towards God."[6]

For the Igbo theologians, like their counterparts in Asia and Latin America, the hermeneutic presuppositions of the West are no longer considered normative in theology[7] or praxis for this kind of seeing or project being advocated for here. As much as the 'theological jargons such as "fulfillment," "ordinary ways," "anonymous Christians," etc., can serve some meaningful purpose for the authentic ministry to which Christians are called, however these jargons cannot fully dispense them of their ministry in today's challenges to authentic Christian witnessing.[8] What we need today more than ever is a Christology of verbs, what Jesus Christ did, rather than a Christology of nouns and adjectives, i.e., what he was.'[9]

In the light of the foregoing, Christians in Igboland are seeking new ways of interpreting not only Scripture but also the human condition in their own cultural and political settings. Even among the Western brethren-theologians today, the hermeneutic enterprise is not restricted to biblical exegesis or the hermeneutics of actual texts. Alongside this; they also advocate the construction of "a hermeneutic of the human world seen from various points of view as text-like, thus permitting a comparative study of the many forms of engagement of the gospel with the human situation."[10]

---

6 Ibid. p. 48.
7 See, J. Moltmann, *Experiences in Theology. Ways and Forms of Christian Theology*, M. Kohl (trans.), Minneapolis, 2000. 'For Jürgen Moltmann, theology always has been – and is for him – not an abstract or otherworldly endeavor but one nourished by, and responsive to, experiences in and with life itself.'
8 See, P. C. Okuma, A *call to authentic living in Christ: The Challenge of the Third Millennium*, Enugu, 1998, p. 4; "...'Christ-Ian': a follower of Christ, a disciple of Christ, a member of the family of Christ, a soldier of Christ, a witness to Christ – by words and deeds (*Eritis mihi testes* – Luke 24:47)."
9 J. Kavunkal, "Ministry and Mission," in J. A. Scherer, & S. B. Bevan, *New Directions in Mission and Evangelization*, Vol. 2, New York, 1994, pp. 91–92.
10 L. S. Mudge, "Hermeneutics" in A. Richardson & J. Bowden (eds.), *The Westminster Dictionary of Christian Theology*, Philadelphia, 1983, p. 253.

In the case of the Igbo,[11] this author tries to develop this through rediscovering of meaning in the social-theological implications of the Eucharist, which is linked with the hermeneutical metanarrative of the 'story of all stories', the resurrection of Christ; in fact it can be said that the latter is the fullness of the former. We relate this as well to how this with reference to the Igbo worldview of 'sacrifice' – celebration as part of body and soul, and as related to living with other humans in the human society. And we relate this as well to how this can serve to sustain the Igbo in this changing time in the faith and fate of humans in the Church, humanity and World Order today.

We reiterate here that the only way of seeing Christians witness truly today to the postmodern situations and challenges in Igboland is for the appropriation of their the Igbo worldview to answer to the demands of the faith and their existential realities. This according to this enquiry is the only way of consolidating Christianity in Igboland in this postmodern era.

We vouchsafe here for the appropriation of 'the Igbo communicative spirit' and hospitality: "The Igbo are nothing if not hospitable. To them hospitality is a major social obligation. Inability to meet it is a humiliating experience for the Igbo. The general complaint of farmers after the planting season concerns the scarcity of yams with which to feed their guests. Hospitality is based on two principles: *direct* reciprocity and *indirect* reciprocity."[12] This can be an agenda for a true and authentic communicativeness and relatedness to other peoples in the world of today as typified too in the sacrament of the Eucharist. This 'relational communicativeness'

---

11 P. C. Okuma, *Towards an African Theology. The Igbo Context in Nigeria*, Brussels, 2002, p. 69. "But suffice it to say that the present Igbo are among the main three tribes in Nigeria, whereas, the other two are Hausa and Yoruba. Majority of the Hausa are Muslims and have their concentration in the Northern part of Nigeria. The Yoruba are mostly Christians too, but live mainly in the Southwestern part of Nigeria. On the other hand, the Igbo are mainly located in what may be called today the Southeastern part of Nigeria, although they are scattered all over the Country, this makes them often victims of the Muslim-Christian Political power game that often manifests itself in Religious riots and mutiny in the Northern part of Nigeria. The Igbo could be said to form the greatest majority of Christians in Nigeria. And could also be found in every part of the world. The Igbo are religious people."
12 V.C. Uchendu, *The Igbo of Southeast Nigeria*, Forth Worth, 1965, p. 71.

becomes too a challenge to theology and spirituality today, towards a better and healthier World Order[13] that is terrorism-free[14] and 'love-full.' This is a key way to 'humanization' of the world – harmony and growth in the Igbo church and society in particular and broadly towards a just society of humans that is free of injustices opened to *Conversation* and authentic witnessing.

In carrying out this onerous project, this has been paged into five chapters here. In the first chapter we go into a transition from the project of the first volume of this book,[15] namely 'theological conversation' into 'witnessing', here showing a brief history of this approach.

In the second chapter, we developed a hermeneutical metanarrative ground for this 'witnessing' – the resurrection of Christ. We call this, in this project, the 'story of stories' because of its central place in Christian faith and narrative. We go further to argue in chapter three that for this witnessing of a people of God, the Igbo need an understanding, an *appropriation* of the worldview of the Igbo. We maintained succinctly that in spite of the low-key place of studying worldview in Western thoughts because of the reasons we adduced in this study, yet, an understanding of the 'worldview' of the Igbo is a key to unraveling the inner recesses of this people, and enhancing the faith in the church and its witnessing today in the society of humankind.

In the fourth chapter we see a spirituality that gives grounding to this 'contextual theology' and its link to the hermeneutics developed here. We consider the Eucharist as this grounding spirituality which if understood via the Igbo idea of sacrifice, celebration and their relevance to the community in witnessing would enhance humankind's spirituality today in this 21st century and redress the problem of human ill-feelings to other humans via terrorism and racism, toward a 'love-full' and truly 'global, peaceable village.'

---

13 H. Kissenger, *World Order*, New York, 2014, p. 2. "Are we facing a period in which forces beyond the restraints of any order determine the future?"
14 Cf. J. Blanchard, *Where was God on September 11?* Darlington, 2002. On 11 September 2001, terrorists hijacked four commercial airliners in the United States.
15 See, Okuma, *Loc. cit.*

Thus, in the final chapter, the Igbo theology is located at the service of God's people and the Igbo society, and the entire human society at large. In this regard issues like enhancing the role of women in witnessing in Igbo church and society, migration, globalization, which cannot be ignored today, the media vis-à-vis politics, and how these affect the Igbo society are addressed toward a better integration of the Igbo into the faith and today's World Order.

Reference is made to the 'self-assisted-industrialized' Nnewi of the South-east of Nigeria and the booming Igbo film industry as typical success cases and efforts at self-reliance that challenges other facets of Igboland – the church and society today and in the future.

Chapter One: The Narrative Behind the Hermeneutics

From the period of the Old Testament into the situation of the early Christians in the New Testament, the lives of peoples have always responded to their faith and belief.

This fact inaugurated in the Old Testament is in alliance with the New Testament. Kwesi A. Dickson gives credence to this when he writes that "the Old Testament has considerable religious value in itself, and on the other, it is inextricably bound up with the New Testament. Hence the Old Testament is brought under the close scrutiny of the New Testament. The implications of this for our topic are clear: the continuity between the Old Testament and African life and thought should be exposed to the cross event, which for Christians is judgment on whatever insight might be gained by looking at the Old Testament and African life and thought together. And the radical nature of the Cross-event spells discontinuity. Yet in this Cross-event Christ's involvement with society is clearly seen; for the nature of the Cross serves to underline the extent to which God would go to identify himself with humankind in the totality of human circumstances."[16]

Thus in the personality of Jesus Christ[17] we see a constant call for faith answering to concrete action – "Give them something to eat!" "Go sell everything you own and distribute the money to the poor, and then come,

---

16 K. A. Dickson, "Continuity and Discontinuity Between the Old Testament and African Life and Thought" in K. Appiah-Kubi & S. Torres, *African Theology en route (papers from the Pan-African Conference of Third World Theologians, Dec 17–23, 1977, Accra, Ghana)*, New York, 1979, p. 107.

17 J. Ukpong, "Christology and Inculturation: A New Testament Perspective" in R. Gibellini, (ed.), *Paths of African Theology*, New York, 1994, pp. 57–58. "The Old Testament law of love of God and neighbor was central for him, and he gave a new and wider interpretation of it. The Ten Commandments, a norm of Christian morality today, is an inheritance from the Old Testament. But Jesus did something new: He revealed the intimate bond between God and humanity that transcends all laws. This may be said to characterize Jesus' approach to evangelization."

follow me"(Lk18, 22).[18] This was also a constant model in the lives of the early Christians in the Acts of the Apostles. The consequence of witnessing to the resurrection of Christ were lives lived out in concrete actions (Acts 4, 32–35). This alludes to 'relatedness' between faith and concrete living. and by elongation, between 'theology' and human existence – calls.[19] As Paul Tillich gives credence to this when he writes that, "faith as ultimate concern is an act of the total personality...it is not a movement of a special section."[20]

---

18 E. katongole, *Beyond Universal Reason. The Relation between Religion and Ethics in the Works of Stanley Hauerwas*, Notre Dame, 2000, p. 192. Katongole argues in favor of Stanley Hauerwas that, "Hauerwas has consistently resisted any suggestions to treat the "social"(political) as something added to the "religious" message of Christ: the Story of Jesus is social and political in itself."

19 P. T. De Chardin, *Le milieu divin essai de vie Intérieure*, Paris, 1957, p. 47, in J. Verstraeten (trans.), in pro manuscripto, *The Rediscovery of Meaning in Professional life: Perspectives for Spirituality of the Laity in the Twenty- first Century*, Leuven, 1999, p. 12. "The experience of the world as milieu divin transforms the secular into a locus of divine presence and in this perspective everything, every aspect of life, even work and business, become sacred for those who distinguish, in each creature and each human activity, an aspect of being attracted to Christ on his way to fulfill the world."

*See also, K. Rahner, Theological Investigations. Man in the Church. Vol. II, K. H. Kruger (transl.), Baltimore, London, 1963, p. 323. "'The world' is not merely constituted by sinful and rebellion opposition to God, Christ, grace and the Church; the world is also God's creation, a reality which can be redeemed and must be sanctified (i.e. the kingdom of God); and even in this respect the world is not simply identical with the Church, but rather the Church is the historically tangible and socially constituted instrument used by Christ for the coming of the kingdom of God through the redemption and sanctification of the world."

*See also, John Paul II, *Christifideles laici*, in Origins. 18, 1989, n. 15 "The term secular must be understood in light of the act of God, the Creator and Redeemer, who has handed over the world to women and to men so that they may participate in the work of creation, free creation from the influence of sin and sanctify themselves in marriage or celibate life, in a family, in a profession and in the various activities of society."

20 P. Tillich, *Dynamics of Faith,* New York, 1957, p. 85. He adds yet that, "Love is an element of faith if faith is understood as ultimate concern. Faith implies love...." *Ibid.* p. 115.

The time of the first Christian Council in Jerusalem (Acts 15) through the different epochs that inaugurated the different Councils in the life of the Church calls for the relatedness of faith to human life, 'from mere *conversation* to authentic witnessing'.[21] The concept of *tria munera* of Vatican II Council, that is, the participation of all the baptized in the priestly, the kingly and prophetic offices of Christ[22] endorses equally this need for 'authentic witnessing' in concrete human situations.

Paradoxically, this fact has been neglected by some 'theologies'. And some that have strived into this area often has been crowned 'Marxist' in orientation and "automatically regarded as the worst possible peril for the church"?[23] Be that as it may, one would not today, vouchsafe for a type of Weberian-Troeltsch legitimating of a specific sort of Christianity whose 'religious' base can be clearly isolated from its 'social' and concrete manifestation call it, 'testimonium' in concrete.[24]

---

21 H. Daniel-Rops, *The Second Vatican Council. The Story behind the Ecumenical Council of Pope John XIII*, A. Guinan (trans.) New York, 1962, p. 28. It is worth noting here that from the period of Nicea Council (325 AD), till Vatican I (1869–1870), twenty councils have taken place: Nicea (325), Constantinople (381), Ephesus (431), Chalcedon (451), Constantinople II (553), Constantinople III (680–681), Nicea II (787), Constantinople VI (869–870), Lateran I (1123), Lateran III (1179), Lateran IV (1215), Lyon I (1245), Lyon II (1274), Vienne (1312), Basel (1437) – (disputed?)[21], Ferrara-Florence (1437–1439), Lateran V (1512–1517), Trent (1543–1563), Vatican I (1869–1870). However, it is disputed as to whether all these councils actually took place. See also, N. P. Tanner, S.J (ed.) *Decrees of the Ecumenical Councils, Vol. II (Trent to Vatican II)*, London, 1990.

22 *Apostolicam Actuositatem*, the decree on the Apostolate of the laity, Art. 2, in N. P. Tanner, SJ (ed.) *Decrees of the Ecumenical Councils, Vol. II (Trent to Vatican II)*, London, 1990. See also, John Paul II, *Christifideles laici: On the Vocation and the Mission of the Lay Faithful in the Church and in the World*, (Vatican translation), Vatican City, 1987, no. 14.

23 J. Sobrino, *The Principle of Mercy: Taking the Crucified People from the Cross*, New York, 1984, p. 118.

24 Katongole, *Loc. cit.*

As we articulated in another book[25] that, a *theological Conversation*[26] is essentially relational.[27] This fact seems most essential for 'theology' and 'theologies' today in this quest to make faith communicative to the people *Sitz im Leben*. We can decipher this clearly in *Gaudium et Spes*, the pastoral constitution of the Church in the Modern World of Vatican II, the Medellin Conference of Latin American bishops and by extension the quest of African Bishops for 'contextual theology' as articulated in their various opinions in the Synod of Bishops for Africa of 1994.

The paradox of the 'unity of theology' in the proclamation and witnessing to the resurrection of Christ and its diversity in the application of this resurrection victory to concrete human situations are realized in 'theologies' – European theology, Liberation theology, Feminists theology, theology of Inculturation and so on. African theology, and indeed 'Igbo theology' in context is a possibility in the light of contextual theologies that answer to the concrete situation of the people. The Igbo have a 'story.'[28] They need theology to address this 'story, through a hermeneutics[29] of

---

25 P. C. Okuma, *Towards an African Theology. The Igbo Context in Nigeria*, Frankfurt, New York, 2002, p. 123.
26 See the Conference tract, "Theology and Conversation. Developing a Relational Theology". Note that this terminology, theological 'Conversation' which was popularized in the 3rd International LEST Congress of Leuven Encounters in Systematic Theology, November 6-9, 2001, aimed at showing that "Relational approaches play an ever more important role as a method in theology and in the elaboration of various systematic subjects. Conversation defines a challenging theological research programme."
27 C. Schwöbel, pro manuscripto, *God as Conversation. Reflections on a Theological Ontology of Communicative Relations*, Leuven, November 7, 2001, p. 2. "Taking the understanding of God as conversation seriously implies that God is eventful, relational, personal, communal and that the divine being is freely communicative being so that the world's being is freely communicated and dependently communicative being."
28 Cf. Basden, G. T. *Among the Ibos of Nigeria*, New York, 1982.
29 K. Mueller-Vollmer, (ed.), *The Hermeneutics Reader*, New York, 1990, p. 2. The term "hermeneutic" occurred sporadically in antiquity; for e.g. it appeared as a title for one of Aristotle's work, *Peri Hermeneias*. In late antiquity hermeneutics the Alexandrian School carried out endeavor. It was also part of the theological culture of the middle Ages. But it was not until the Reformation and after that that "hermeneutics" as a special discipline came into being.

'appropriation' of Igbo values which would be based in understanding the Igbo worldview.

This is important as one notices that, throughout the history of Christian theology, there has been diversity in theological hermeneutics and differing "schools" of interpretation – from the Alexandrian and Antiochene schools of late antiquity to the new hermeneutics and Frankfurt schools in the Western world and EATWOT in the Third world of the twentieth century. The contemporary theological scene is indeed saturated with diverse hermeneutic approaches and perspectives.[30] Of course the use of interpretation poses a great problem among scholars. Paul Ricoeur attests that, "there is no general hermeneutics, no universal canon for exegesis, but only disparate and opposed theories concerning the rules on interpretation."[31] This is because of divergences of peoples, and more so, because of the needs of peoples.

There is a need to make the faith evergreen in witnessing in the concrete situation of the Igbo in Nigeria today. This is both a prospect and a great challenge. This needs a specific hermeneutics that moves away from mere 'conversations' to 'concrete witnessing'. This is the prospect of Igbo theology in context. It is capable of becoming a discipline and so able to enter into dialogue and conversations with other theologies. However, from a terminological point of view, 'witness' is preferable to these more fashionable expressions because witness preserve the realization that, while contact with others may sometimes take the form of explicit argument and dialogue, the more primary form of hermeneutical contact is the mere presence of another – which leads to a 'display' of the richness of practices and character made possible by the other's particular story. In other words, the primary hermeneutical challenge is not 'listen' to what the other has to say, but to 'see' who the other is, without attempting to reduce the other to an extension of one's self-understanding.'[32]

---

30 E. Martey, *African Theology: Inculturation and Liberation*, New York, 1993, p. 54.
31 P. Ricoeur, *Freud and Philosophy. An Essay on Interpretation*, Connecticut, 1970, p. 26.
32 S. Hauerwas, *After Christendom*, Nashville, 1991, p. 159.

'Witness' carries an immediate association with this normative aspect of peaceableness in a way that dialogue and conversation do not as such. Dialogue and conversation may tend to obscure the epistemological preoccupation of witness; dialogue by its association with political compromise, and conversation by the liberal aestheticization of communication. Witness, however, is primarily a reminder that the peaceful presence of others is essential for the very conception of historical truth.'[33] And what historical truth, if one may enquire? For our context here, this historical truth is the resurrection of Christ, the 'story of all stories' whose hermeneutics challenges towards 'faith engaging faith' and 'faith engaging existential engagement' of a people in concrete situation through insight into the worldview of the people.

This hermeneutics is what we call 'a metanarrative,' the resurrection of Christ – 'the story of all stories.'[34] This 'story of all stories' has its implication for each people's story seen through the 'worldview' of the people in relation to 'a theology.' As Lesslie Newbigin opines that, "if our model of truth is embodied in a story, a story of which we are ourselves a part, then the only available form of knowledge is by faith in the One who is the author of the story. We are part of the story.... It follows that the only way in which we can affirm the truth and therefore the authority of the gospel is by preaching it, by telling the story, and by our corporate living of the story in the life and worship of the church...it means that

---

33 E. Katongole, *Beyond Universal Reason. The Relation Between Religion and Ethics in the Work of Stanley Hauerwas*, Notre Dame, 2000, p. 173.

34 *Ibid.* p. 155. "All our actions and rational inquiry are so tradition-dependent that there is no way one can step outside historical traditions to come into a direct and immediate contact with reality. There is no 'theory of truth' as such – no story of stories that would guarantee the truthfulness of other stories. There are only particular configurations of reality, particular stories and canons of rationality, which are themselves tradition-dependent." But this writer here differs in a way from Katongole. The resurrection of Christ is deployed here as the 'story of stories' in the sense that in this 'Christ-story' is embedded the 'story of humanity' – our story is embedded in the Christ story consummated in his victory, that of his resurrection which is also our own victory. This Christ story also challenges us as the fundament for our witnessing as Christians. See, Obilor, J.I., The Doctrine of the Resurrection of the Dead and the Igbo Belief in the "Reincarnation", Frankfurt am Main, Berlin, New York, 1993.

we affirm that truth is to be found only in the personal commitment to a life of discipleship with Him who is himself the truth. We have to tell and enact the story."[35] This project is about enacting this evergreen truth, the resurrection of Christ. Telling the story of a people through entering their worldview in the light of this evergreen 'story of stories.'

In spite of the fact that the issue of worldview is mostly overlooked by Western scholarship for the reasons we shall give in this work, yet it is worth placing emphasis on the importance of worldview in breaking into the recesses of the Igbo, as a way of understanding their narrative, their story – their history as a people, even before the coming of the early missionaries. The appropriation of this could help in living the hermeneutical metanarrative, the resurrection of Christ, 'the story of all stories' in the quest for making the faith of the people and their concrete *Sitz im leben* 'existential,'[36] – the greatest challenge in this age for Christianity!

In this relationality of witnessing, 'the Igbo theology' is a possibility in the light of contextual theologies that answer to the concrete situation of the people. These concrete situations of the Igbo today in the local churches and in the society raise questions. That challenges to better ways of the relational nature of the faith in witnessing to concrete situations in this era of Postmodernity with its so-called 'sensibilities.'[37]

Accordingly in the words of David N. Power, we cannot overlook the "current cultural reality."[38] The so-called post-modern character of our contemporary culture affects the religious tradition and how that tradition can meaningfully address such a post-modern world[39] is very important for every people. Since, according to Donald G. Bloesch, "Something else

---

35 L. Newbigin, *Truth and Authority in Modernity*. (In the series, "Christian Mission and Modern Culture"), Pennsylvania, 1996, pp. 80–81.
36 See, J. F. Koelber, *Vatican II and Phenomenology. Reflections on the Life-World of the Church*, Dordrecht, Boston, Lancaster, 1985.
37 P. Lakeland, *Postmodernity. Christian Identity in a Fragmented Age*, Minneapolis, 1997, p. 113.
38 D. N. Power, *Sacrament: The Language of God's Giving*, New York, 1999, p. 12.
39 Lakeland, *Op. cit.* p. ix; See also, G. De Schrijver, s.j. "Sacramentaliteits van Het Bestaan in de Overgang van Premoderniteit naar Moderniteit en PostModerniteit, in J. Lamberts, *Hedendaagse Accenten in de Sacramentologie,* Leuven, 1994, pp. 17–64.

is happening in our century. The gods are being reborn. When God is dead, the way is open for the return of the gods of pre-Christian times, the gods of volk, blood, sex, and soil. The Enlightenment desacralised the heavens; now society and nature are becoming the new domains of the sacred."[40] How can a people sustain faith and existential engagement in this time and situation today? The need for Igbo theology making the faith alive and relational in the people's existential situation becomes of utmost importance. A type of theology and spirituality that will answer to faith and hope for humans in the Igbo society today are urgent for the Igbo and the human society in general.

This takes into cognizance of the fact that, "theology in the period of modernity has been largely captive to academic institutions that are controlled by the assumptions of modernity. In such institutions it is customary to hear that what is being taught is to be distinguished from what is called "confessional" theology. The implication is that, in contrast to what is done in the church there is offered here a "scientific" account of the matters with which theology deals. Once again we are dealing with modern illusion of a kind of objectivity from which the personal commitment of the knowing subject has been eliminated. The temptation for some Christians is simply to stop their ears against this and to develop another kind of objectivity based on a doctrine of scriptural inerrancy. But this is no solution. What has to be done is to affirm the story as the clue to all understanding and to engage the academic world in dialogue that openly challenges the assumptions of modernity."[41]

We are not mere concerned with the so-called "academic theology" which is very important too as 'a tool of witnessing today,' (since one cannot have a good practice without an adequate and substantiated theory) but we go further across this academic domain into the twin partner of 'communicative relation' of *theological Conversation* that matures in *Witnessing* in concrete. But in doing this we intend to go into furthering and deepening what is called in this volume the 'hermeneutical metanarrative', the resurrection of Christ as the fulcrum of the Igbo theology and to see

---

40 D. G. Bloesch, *Crumbling Foundations. Death & Rebirth In An Age of Upheaval,* Michigan, 1984, p. 38.
41 Lesslie, *Op. cit.* pp. 82–83.

its communicativeness to the gospel witnessing in the concrete situation of the people and making the faith alive and existential in the light of their quest for a self-reliant church, a more 'humane humanity' and a better World Order since after September 11.[42]

---

[42] J. Blanchard, *Where was God On September 11?* Darlington, Massachusetts, 2002. pp. 3–31; "On 11 September 2001, terrorists hijacked four commercial airlines in the United States. Two were rammed into the twin towers of the World Trade Center in New York City and a third into the Pentagon in Washington, DC. Passengers on the fourth plane fought with the hijackers, but it crashed in Pennsylvania with the loss of all on board. In most devastating terrorist attack in history, the world's tallest building had been reduced to rubble and some 3, 000 people blasted or crushed to death. The Times called it 'The day that changed the modern world'. Another newspaper claimed, 'History will never be the same again.' In a CNN Time Warner poll taken three months later, 73% of those interviewed said, 'It has changed everything for ever.' As the media teemed with speculation as to how such a thing could have happened, and what the repercussions might be, people were asking one inescapable question: Where was God on September 11? The answer may surprise you...." (Back cover quote).

Chapter Two: The Story of All Stories: The Resurrection of Christ!

"But you can't go barefoot!" Vladimir says to Estragon. "But Christ did" replies Estragon to his challenger. "Christ! 'What's Christ got to do with it? You're not going to compare yourself to Christ.'" Reiterates Vladimir. "All my life I've compared myself to him." Replies Estragon.[43] What's Christ resurrection got to do with 'hermeneutics and metanarrative' some might ask? It is not totally out of context that some might pursue the same question further, what has the hermeneutical metanarrative of Christ's resurrection got to do with the Igbo existential living in the church and in the world today as 'a people of God'? What has Christ got to do with it? What has His resurrection victory got to do with the faith of a people?[44] Part of the reason is the fact that this people, the African – the Igbo as 'a people of God' are seriously connected to the 'historicality of the biblical texts.'[45] If the resurrection of Christ is real and indeed it is, then, in the final analysis it must be perceived as acting in some way in or upon the history of the

---

43 S. Beckett, *Waiting for Godot. A Tragicomedy in Two Acts*, London, 2000, p. 66. This play first published in 1952 by Les editions de minuit, now done in hardcover by the Folio Society London (2000 edition) as 'controversial' as this play is, however, narrates Beckett's experiences during the World wars.
44 Die Deutschen Bischöfe, "Jesu Leben, sein Tod und seine Auferstehung als Anfang des wahren Friedens" in *Gerechter Friede*, no. 66, 27. September 2000, Bonn, pp. 26–31.
45 P. Lakeland, *Postmodernity. Christian Identity in a Fragmented Age*, Minneapolis, 1997, p. 41. "Theologies in postmodernity try to find their way between two familiar extremes. At one end lies the liberal dissolution of the specificity of Christianity and a thorough accommodation to the world, often masked by a turn to the pietistic or the emotional that in the end cedes the realm of intellect to secular wisdom. At the other end lie fideisms, both biblical and ecclesial. But the world between the two extremes is anything but familiar, a strange landscape of poststructuralists, deconstructionists, chaos theorists, and entropy junkies, struggling for conceptual or metaphorical control over a bewilderingly complex world and a stunningly vast profusion of data. The theologies that emerge from this task bear the mask more of temperament than ideology: there are the timid, the devil-may-care, and the pragmatic, and this in itself is enough to label all of them "postmodern."

people of God.[46] Do most 'theologies' not begin with historical experiences of a people?

In this regard, some theologians and thinkers (especially those of postmodernity) might decide to shift grounds to the Trinitarian Christological dimension of Christian reality[47] in the world today as a possible option of *relational communication* in *theological Conversation*. In this regard, D'Costa will argue that the normativity of a "Trinitarian Christology,"[48] protects against exclusivism and pluralism, enabling both a pneumatologically driven attention to "the universal activity of God in the history of humankind," revealing love of neighbor (including those of other religions) as "an imperative for all Christians," and licensing praxis and dialogue.[49]

Some others would tend towards 'God's motherhood' as a hermeneutical point of departure and so on. However, there is a connectedness between the Trinitarian Christology and the Christ's event – the Resurrection, which is our focus for a unique Igbo theology hermeneutics. This follow from the fact that, the Resurrection of Christ is "A Work of the Holy Trinity"[50] and

---

46 See, Edward Farley, *Divine Empathy: A Theology of God*, Minneapolis, 1996. This erudite text focused on the fact of God's acting.
47 See, T. Merrigan & J. Haers, (eds.), *The Myriad Christ. Plurality and the Quest for Unity in Contemporary Christology*, Leuven, 2000. In this academic compendium, a whole range of scholars from different cultural background discussed the issue of Christology as it applies to their unique situation. However, Terrence Merrigan in his article in this compendium titled, "The historical Jesus in the Pluralist theology of Religions",(pp. 63–65), raises the engaging discussion between two tendencies in the theory of Christology namely exclusivism and inclusivism and their dangers.
48 For different current African approaches to the issue of Christology and Inculturation, See, J.S. Ukpong, "Christology and Inculturation: A New Testament Perspective" in R. Gibellini (ed.), *Paths of African Theology*, New York, 1994, pp. 40–61. In this work, Ukpong treats the different approaches to clarifying the meaning of Jesus in relation to Inculturation.
49 Gavin D'costa, *The Classic*, Cambridge, 1983, pp. 138–141.
50 The Catechism of the Catholic Church, (Vatican City, 1992), the edition used here is the English translation, Pauline Publications African, Kenya, 1995, p. 180. "Christ's Resurrection is an object of faith in that it is a transcendent intervention of God himself in creation and history. In it the three divine persons act together as one, and manifest their own proper characteristics. The Father's power "raised up" Christ his Son and by doing so perfectly introduced his Son's humanity, including his body, into the Trinity. Jesus is conclusively

this has meaning and saving significance[51] in concrete for the Church, for humans and for the World Order.

The love, which inspires the life of the Trinity and the offering of Christ of himself for the life of the world, which culminates in his Resurrection, both inseparable realities hinge on love as Self-sacrifice and as the ultimate connecting factor.[52]

Is *theological Conversation* today not in a sense like 'Waiting for Godot?' A fall back to unique experiences! Think in the light of the French revolution[53] and concomitant development of thoughts and theologies till today. Are most of our experiences in the world today not almost like 'Waiting for Godot' in a way? We could as well raise more alarm, what has Christ got to do with it? Even in doing Theology today as during the Enlightenment period that valorized the subject and then emerged the autonomous secular realm, while this was to some degree the product of the Reformation, however it represents as it would to theology today (in postmodernity), an enormous challenge to Christianity and her narratives.[54]

If Christianity is to survive and the faith of peoples, it could no longer live quite so unreflectively today without letting her treasured narratives answer in concrete to the faith of 'the people of God.'[55] It seems

---

revealed as "Son of God in power according to the Spirit of holiness by his Resurrection from the dead." St Paul insists on the manifestation of God's power through the working of the Spirit who gave life to Jesus' dead humanity and called it to the glorious state of Lordship."

51 *Ibid.* pp. 181–182.
52 Marie-Joseph Nicolas, *Théologie de la resurrection. Jesus la resurrection et la vie,* Toulouse, 1982, p. 389. "Au-delà de'obeissance, de l'offrande, du sacrifice, l'amour qui les inspire, secret ultime de la vie Trinitaire et de l'aime humaine du Christ, régnera sur le monde de la résurrection."
53 See, Thomas Carlyle, *The French Revolution. A History*, Volume I (The Bastille), Volume II (The Constitution,), Volume III (The Guillotine) London, 1837, (Reprinted. 2001, The Folio Society, London). A keen survey and reading of these voluminous historical compendium will bring to perspective the French Revolution and it's after effects even till today in the way people think and even their attitude towards the faith. All never became the same after this unique experience in Europe.
54 Lakeland, *Op. cit.* pp. 39–41.
55 It is worth noting that with the dawn of the ecclesiology of 'the people of God' as drawn up by the Council Fathers in Lumen Gentium of Vatican II, a different

paradoxical, to say that no matter tribe and tongue may differ, but in the unity of the reality of her narratives namely, the resurrection of Christ all Christians stand.[56] As Hans Urs von Balthasar says, "Rightly enough, the event of the resurrection has always been emphasized that there can have been no witnesses to the event of the Son's resurrection by the Father – anymore than there can to the act of the incarnation. And yet the two actions are foundational events of a Salvation which is for man, and God does not bring about these events without man anymore than he allowed the passion to happen without human cooperation."[57]

---

understanding and approach to mission of the Church and her people took a different turn and shape. See, G. Alberigo, 'The Christian Situation After Vatican II: Phenomenology and History of the Postconciliar Period,' In G. Alberigo, J-P. Jossua, and J. A. Komonchak (eds.), transl. by M.J.O'connell, *The Reception of Vatican II*, Washington D.C., 1987, pp. 1–2. For the erudite Vatican II historian, Giuseppe Alberigo, the Vatican II Council was essentially, " "open" to the other Christian confessions and to a variety of cultural influences; it also aimed at restoring both a real subordination of ecumenical councils to the word of God and real involvement in human history, to the point even of recognizing in this history "signs" pregnant with the gospel. To that extent, Vatican II represents a recovery of directions – neglected but not abandoned– that are profoundly imbedded in Christian tradition as understood in its fullest Catholic sense:" *Furthermore, this writer agrees with Alberigo that, "In fact, Roncalli's vocabulary "pastoral" was an exceptionally rich term and undoubtedly referred to the highest level of the Church's life. By using this adjective, then, he was giving Vatican II an ecclesial scope that was not solely dogmatic or solely disciplinary but all embracing." *Ibid*. p. 17.

56 S. Hauerwas, *The Peaceable Kingdom: A Primer in Christian Ethics*, Notre Dame, 1983, p. 120. Talking about faith and theology, Hauerwas wrote that, "If we have a foundation it is the story of Christ." Of course postmodernity that focuses on pluralism would challenge us in this regard of the 'appropriateness of presenting religious or ethical vision as universally relevant in an intensely pluralistic world' (See, Lakeland, *Op. cit*. p. 59), for our 'contextual theology' project. But we would underscore yet in this regard by reasserting that the metanarrative of Christ's resurrection remains our traditional Christian patrimony, belief and value that stands for all times and in all ages. Of course this posture does not extricate us from dialogue but 're-visions us' to deploy the world of Stanley Hauerwas for theological Conversation with other theologies.

57 H. Urs von Balthasar, *Mysterium Paschale: The Mystery of Easter*, Aidan Nichols (translated), Michigan, 1990, p. 249.

Be that as it may it is paradoxical to say that the challenge of contemporary Christian religious thought and theology today are to keep alive in the postmodern world a religious vision created in a distantly premodern cultural context, honed to a level of sophistication and lived out courageously through many centuries of premodernity and even see how that is to be realized within a people's *weltanschauung* today. Whether the task is thought of primarily as one of reception or of mediation, there is no gainsaying its reality. We may struggle to find contemporary language and symbols in which the gospel message can be expressed (mediation), or we may determine that the community of faith needs to purify its capacity to hear once again the Christian story in its biblical transparency (reception), but we cannot deny that either path constitutes a challenge.[58] It is this challenge that calls for an *appropriation*[59] of this Christian patrimony, the hermeneutical metanarrative of Christ's resurrection for the realization of the ideals and the *Sitz im leben* of 'the people of God,' namely, the Igbo.

Once again one may reiterate the question, what has these got to do with Christ? What has this got to do with a theology in context? The question goes on and on. 'Never stop questioning' says Albert Einstein. After all this is the stuff of theological Conversation – 'relational communication,' and the way to live today in a pluralistic society and a unique Church that is opened to the World and Cultures in dialogue.[60]

The appropriation of the hermeneutical metanarrative of this Christian patrimony, 'the resurrection of Christ' as the base of a 'contextual theology' is what we see implicit in the personality of Paul, the apostle of the Gentiles and not only on him but on the Corinthian church and in fact on

---

58 *Loc. cit.*
59 P. Ricoeur, *Hermeneutics and the human sciences*, trans and edited by J.B. Thompson, New York, 1980, p. 182. "'Appropriation' is the key idea, which governs the methodology of interpretation."
60 Of course this is one of the greatest achievements of the 1965 document of the Second Vatican Council, the Pastoral Constitution on the Church in the Modern World (*Gaudium et Spes*) with its 'openness'. See, Y. Congar, The role of the Church in the Modern world in H. Vorgrimler, (eds.), et al. Commentary on the Documents of Vatican II (Vol. V). *Pastoral Constitution on the Church in the Modern World*, New York, 1969, p. 204. NB: Congar questions in this regard: 'what justification does the Church offer for its activity which goes beyond the work of conveying to the faithful the Easter grace of renewal?'

all believers.⁶¹ This metaphor or metanarrative is developed further in the Pauline concept of reconciliation through the God's saving work in Christ, through His resurrection in which He now reconciled humanity back to God, which challenges Christians to a fellowship in witnessing in the concrete. According to Seyoon Kim, 'Pauline metaphor or metanarrative of reconciliation grew out of his own theological reflections on his Damascus road conversion experience, in which for Paul through Christ's atonement via His death and completed in his resurrection we are reconciled to God, as by His eucharistic saying about the blood of the covenant poured out for the forgiveness of sins' (this eucharistic aspect and its implication for the Igbo will be discussed in detailed in Chapter Five).⁶²

Accordingly, if the above thesis is correct, the way in which Paul developed this biblical metaphor or metanarrative has a paradigmatic significance for our theologizing today. For each people and personal experiences of encounter with the risen Christ either through the 'missionary Christianity' or otherwise, challenge to a deeper integration of these experiences, of making it ones own within one's context that which has been wrought for all humanity, the victory of Christ's resurrection (here our operational word, *appropriation* as used by Paul Ricoeur as it refers to a 'text', which we nuanced in the first volume of our book mentioned above applies).⁶³

The truth of the matter is that this 'apostolic kerygma', the resurrection metanarrative will have to be interpreted by means of a new category drawn from a people's experience, thereby making the kerygma more relevant to our situation today as a people of God.⁶⁴

---

61 See, R. Bieringer, "Death and Resurrection of Christ. Effects on all" in Notes on Pauline interaction with the Corinthians, (part III, V), Leuven, *unpublished lecture notes,* 2001. The meaning of the resurrection of Christ could be read into the Pauline corpus especially, 2Cor 5:14–21. The effect of this is not only on the personality of Paul but also on the Corinthians, on all.

62 S. Kim, "God Reconciled His Enemy to Himself: The Origin of Paul's Concept of Reconciliation" in Richard N. Longenecker (edited), *The Road from Damascus. The Impact of Paul's Conversion on His life, Thought, and Ministry,* Michigan, Cambridge, 1997, pp. 102, 122. According to Kim, "In this way, the metaphor of reconciliation, which is one of the most significant categories of preaching the gospel of Christ, came into being." *Ibid.* p. 123.

63 Okuma, *Towards an African Theology,* pp. 83–84.

64 S. Kim, *Loc. cit.*

At the same time one cannot overlook also the difficulties that accompany such appropriation, of bringing a foreign reader that is perhaps biased about 'the text of operation or the context of operation' to conviction. While the 'concept of text' is problematic in Ricoeur but 'text' here is to be understood in the sense of his use as that which is there and challenges one. Thus 'Text' in the words of Jacques Haers while interpreting Ricoeur, "refers more clearly to the receptive and creative dynamism of the hermeneutical process of appropriation."[65] Of course here lack of total conviction of the foreigner to the text of use would not mean total absence of conviction. In this regard the statement of Martha Nussbaum is quite *ad rem*, "excellence is impossible without vulnerability."[66] 'Vulnerability' itself is even the key to success and perspicacity for 'a theology'. 'Theology so understood this way too, becomes a link to praxis, fulfils a prophetic function insofar as it interprets historical events of a people with the intention of revealing and proclaiming their profound meaning. Accordingly, the hermeneutics of the resurrection of Christ consists especially in making the world a better place and making Christians at home in the church within their culture. Only in this way can one be able to discover what the resurrection of Christ means to a people's hermeneutical metanarrative of the Gospel for their existence as a people of God.'[67]

---

65 J. Haers, "A Risk Observed," in T. Merrigan, (ed.), Louvain Studies 21(1996), p. 47.
66 M. Nussbaum, *The Fragility of Goodness*, New York, 1986, (5, 15). Of course one has to read this Nussbaum phraseology in the context of her essentialism, in which she assumes to deal with constant 'human' problems, which have not changed over the centuries. Of course these have also their implications with the 'liberal cultural elite.' This is not our meaning of use here; rather, this quote is to be taken in its 'first-face meaning' as a metaphor with deep rooted metanarrative meaning.
67 G. Gutierrez, *A Theology of Liberation*, London, 1978, p. 11. Here Gutierrez reflects the idea of Schillebeeckx. See also, P. Ricoeur, *Hermeneutics and the Human Sciences*, edited and translated by. J. B. Thompson, Cambridge, 1980, p. 1. "The nature of language and meaning, of action, interpretation and subjectivity, are issues of increasing concern to a wide range of contemporary disciplines."

Here we have a theology that answers to a people's *existential engagement*.[68] Which is made possible courtesy of the 'world of the biblical metanarrative'. In this way the 'hermeneutics of biblical metanarratives' perspective has double influence that of integration, stimulation and critical functions on one hand, on the other that of motivating the role of a people to give answer to their faith in concrete.[69] Accordingly as a specifically poetic 'world' the biblical text generates a metamorphosis in its readers, which enables them (and their communities) to interpret their lives in a new light. Biblical metanarratives like that of the resurrection of Christ puts a people's faith to new and particular perspective, that of an abundant economy of grace and love – the redeemed, that calls for appropriation in concrete. In the words of Vaclav Havel this responsibility is "the pen with which we write the story of the world's new creation in the history of being."

For the Igbo this hermeneutical metanarrative key is a pen on hand to tell their story, the story of their faith, their belief, the reality of their world as a people in the concreteness and realities of the continent in all its divergences, of their local church the way it is today and how they wish it to be, of their history of being as a people today and what they wish to become in the future.

According to Johan Verstraeten, 'the biblical poesis has this possibility for the development of an imaginative space for experiments of thought in concrete.[70] This is *au courant* with the fact that biblical imagination influences concrete acts as "first laboratories".[71] Such an imagination

---

68 J. Verstraeten, *Beyond Business Ethics: Leadership, Spirituality and the Quest for Meaning*, Unpublished lecture, Leuven, 2000, p. 8 "The experience of the world as milieu divin transforms the secular into a locus of divine presence and in this perspective everything, every aspect of life, even work and business, become sacred for those who distinguish, in each creature and each human activity, an aspect of being attracted to the fulfillment of the world."

69 J. Verstraeten, The "'World' of the Bible as Meta-Ethical Framework of Meaning for Ethics: An Interpretation," in Hendrik M. Vroom & Jerald D. Gort (eds.), *Holy Scriptures in Judaism, Christianity and Islam. Hermeneutics, Values and Society*, Amsterdam/Atlanta, 1997, p. 139.

70 Verstraeten, The "'World' of the Bible..."*Ibid.* p. 143.

71 P. Ricoeur, *Soi-même comme un autre (l'ordre philosophique)*, Paris 1990, pp. 167, 200. See especially, P. Ricoeur, *Time and Narrative* (3 Volumes),

enables Christians, a people to look at the world and at life through his or her eyes (*voir comme*) and it enables them also to discover new ways of being and new models of action (*agir comme*). When a people have identified themselves imaginatively with Christ's resurrection, they can transform the 'self' into a 'christomorphic self'.[72] This has nothing to do with servile imitation or a mimesis as described by René Girard.[73] Instead, this hermeneutical metanarrative reaches out into an imaginatively mediated mystical 'acting as they would' leading not only to a radicalization and humanization of their Christian attitudes, but also to an acceptance of the scandal of the cross that led to the resurrection of Christ, epitomized in self-sacrificing love that challenges a people.

This hermeneutical metanarrative being advocated for here would enable the Igbo to demythologize some of her traditional values and culture as 'strange' toward an authentic appropriation and to overcome some of its ideological distortions about politics and the society, and even become an enhancement to entering into dialogue with other religions, theologies and the rest of humanity.[74]

Kathleen McLaughlin & David Pellauer (translated), Chicago, 1984–1988. Here Ricouer develops most formidable philosophical arguments for narratives.

72 Verstraeten, *Op. cit.* 144. See also, Lawrence Boadt & Mark S. Smith (eds.), *Imagery and Imagination in Biblical Essays in Honor of Aloysius Fitzgerald*, F.S.C. (The Catholic Biblical Quarterly Monograph, Series 32), Washington, 2000. Although this text is essentially concerned with collections that deal with the Old Testament books, however it gives clue as to the power of imagery and imagination in the biblical literature.
73 See, René Girard, *Le bouc émissaire*, Paris, 1982.
74 *Ibid.* Pp. 144–145.

It is paradoxical to say that Vatican II Council, the 'ecumenical Council'[75] par excellence gave priority of place to biblical narratives and metaphors as hermeneutical foundations in her 16 documents.[76] Foremost ecclesial theologians like Augustine,[77] Don Scotus, Peter Abelard, Thomas Aquinas, and later ones like Karl Rahner,[78] Karl Barth,[79] M-D Chenu, Yves Congar,[80] Gerard Philips,[81] Hans Urs von Balthasar,[82] Edward Schillebeeckx,[83]

---

75 Y. Congar, "A Last look at the Council" in *Vatican II by Those Who Were There*, Alberic Stacpole(ed), London, 1986, p. 344. "The Second Vatican Council was an ecumenical Council in the technical sense of the word. It was also open to the other two forms of ecumenicity in its dynamic understanding of the Church. This is clear from a reading of the very first lines of *Lumen Gentium*, its chapter on the People of God, its idea of the Church as the 'sacrament of Salvation' and the words subsist in that occur in section 8 of the text. These words affirm the authenticity of the Roman Catholic Church of Christ and the Apostles without devaluing the obviously different ecclesial quality of the other Christian Communion."
76 See, N. P. Tanner, S.J., (ed.) *Decrees of the Ecumenical Councils*, Vol. II (Trent to Vatican II), London, 1990. Especially the document, Dei Verbum, the Dogmatic Constitution on Divine Revelation. While the Church had historically laid credence to tradition and authority of the Scriptures in teaching, it is equally arguable as to whether the Protestant Reformation and her focus on Solus Scriptura that partly inaugurated the Council of Trent had heightened this endeavor in the following period, the so called 'Catholic counter-Reformation.' However, the Second Vatican II remains the Church's foremost effort to rediscovery of her patrimony of the Scriptures and biblical hermeneutics in teaching.
77 See, Allan D. Fitzgerald, O.S.A.(ed), *Augustine Through the Ages: An Encyclopedia*, Michigan, Cambridge, 1999.
78 K. Rahner, *Theological Investigations: Man in the Church*, vol. 11, K-H, Kruger, (translated), Baltimore, London, 1963.
79 See, Mueller David.l. *Foundation of Karl Barth's Doctrine of Reconciliation, Jesus Christ Crucified and Risen* (Toronto Studies in Theology, 54), 1991.
80 Y. M-J. Congar, *Jalons pour une théologie du laïcat*, Unam Sanctam 23, Paris, 1953.
81 G. Philips, *The Role of the Laity in the Church*, J.R.Gilbert and J.W. Moudry (trans.), Cork, 1955.
82 H. Urs von Balthasar, *Mysterium Paschale: The Mystery of Easter*, Aidan Nichols (translated), Michigan, 1990.
83 E. Schillebeeckx, *Christ: The Experience of Jesus As Lord*, John Bowden (translated), New York, 1989.

Joseph Cardinal Ratzinger,[84] Gustav Gutierrez,[85] Jon Sobrino,[86] Leonardo Boff,[87] John Milbank,[88] John Hick and Paul Knitter,[89] Gavin D'Costa[90] and a host of others, submitted to some kind of biblical hermeneutical narratives in their theologies.[91]

Does this kind of development that is more vintage of postmodernity scholarship not lead us to a question of nuances? While there are those who would argue that utilizing the Christian tradition as the lens through

---

84 Joseph Kardinal Ratzinger, *Salz der Erde. Christentum und Katholische Kirche an der Jahrtausendwende Ein Gesprach mit Peter Seewald*, Stuttgart, 1998.
85 G. Gutierrez, *A Theology of Liberation*, London, 1978.
86 J. Sobrino, *The Principle of Mercy. Taking the Crucified People from the Cross*, New York, 1984.
87 L. Boff, *Jesus Christ Liberator. A Critical Christology for Our Time*, New York, 1981, p. 7ff. In this text he handles among other things the conflicting theories on the Christ of faith and the Historical Jesus.
88 John Milbank, *Theology and Social Theory*, Cambridge, 1991. In this work, Milbank straddles the issues and debates of postmodernity in a highly idiosyncratic reading of Western civilization.
89 John Hick And Paul Knittter (eds.), *The Myth of Christian Uniqueness: Toward a Pluralistic Theology of Religions*, New York, 1987.
90 Gavin D'costa (ed.), *Christian Uniqueness Reconsidered: The Myth of a Pluralistic Theology of Religions*, New York, 1990, p.x. This second volume rejects the notion of a pluralistic theology and explores whether "Christian claims concerning uniqueness (are) coherent and sustainable and even illuminated in making sense of religious plurality." Of course this book was in response to a former collection edited by, John Hick And Paul Knittter (eds.), *The Myth of Christian Uniqueness: Toward a Pluralistic Theology of Religions*, New York, 1987, p.viii. this text focused on a "move away from insistence on the superiority or finality of Christ and Christianity toward recognition of the independent validity of other ways."
91 E. Katongole, *Beyond Universal Reason. The Relation between Religion and Ethics in the Work of Stanley Hauerwas*, Indiana, 2000, p. 105. "Within theology, "narrative theology" has been characterized by the same wide and nouniform (sic) appeal to narrative, ranging from an explication of religion in human experience in general to the use of narrative as a heuristic category for explicating the basic substance of Christian theology, from focus on biography (and even autobiography) as a way of displaying Christian convictions to a hermeneutics of biblical narrative." See, Michael Goldberg, *Theology and Narrative: A critical Introduction*, Nashville, 1982. This text is a good introduction to the trends of narrative theology.

which I interpret the world and encounter other religions is an inevitable hermeneutical circumscription, the so-called 'scandal of particularity' revisited, as it were. On the other we find those who, while accepting this inevitability, would like also to talk in terms of the normativity of Christianity, while recognizing that the incommensurability of other traditions prevents any easy descent into inclusivisim. They are, in a typically postmodern move, content to live with the ambiguity.[92]

Apart from exposing the theological highlights of some of these arguments, however, the effort here is not opting for 'pluralism' in the way Panikkar and his supporters would argue.[93] However our effort is geared toward the *appropriation* of Christian patrimony as a hermeneutics for the Igbo in authentic witnessing in concrete and making the faith more integral in their existential situation. For this writer, the hermeneutical metanarrative of the resurrection of Christ is most august for a theology as 'contextual theology' being suggested here. Since the Igbo need "the privileged means by which we reconfigure our confused, unformed, and ...mute temporal existence."[94] And there is the need to do this through authentic appropriation of their cultural values and traditions,[95] through depicting their identity as a people of God by appropriating their values to answer authentically to the content of their Christian convictions and for witnessing for the faith in concrete. For the victory of Christ's resurrection won for humankind is equally won for them as a people of God and this needs to be appropriated – 'made ones own' to use the phraseology of Ricoeur.

---

92 Lakeland, *Op. cit.* p. 81.
93 R. Panikkar, "The Jordan, the Tiber and the Ganges," in John Hick And Paul Knittter (eds.), *Op. cit.* p. 109.
94 P. Ricoeur, Time and Narrative, Vol. I, K. McLaughlin & D. Pellauer (translated), Chicago, 1984, p. xi.
95 MacIntyre, A. *After Virtue. A Study in Moral Theory*, (second edition), London, 1997, p. 206. "Our initiation into a story as well as the ability to sustain ourselves in that story depends on others who have gone before and those who continue to travel with us. "What I am, therefore, is in key part what I inherit, a specific past that is present to some degree in my present. I find myself part of a history and that is generally to say, whether I like it or not, whether I recognize it or not, one of the bearers of a tradition."

The Igbo 'as a people were dead and have come back to life, were lost and are found by Christ (Luke 15, 31-32).' Their checked history[96] and even today the situations in the local churches and in the entire continent of Africa are concrete evidence on one hand and on the other the uncertainties of the future in their local churches (with the astronomical increase in priestly and religious vocations, other substantial realities),[97] in the continent's economy, general socio-political situation in Nigeria in particular and in the world in general with the incident of September 11.

In spite of these, this people's quest for a self-reliant church that looks to the future with hope, that nourishes the faith making it evergreen in the land make this reality of 'a unique contextual theology' foreseeable. With such a 'hermeneutical metanarrative' being discussed here and such a theological project being worked out here, they would be capable of meeting other theologies on their grounds – entering into theological Conversation with them and at the same time giving deeper meaning and answering adequately and integrally to the Igbo as members of the people of God.

---

96 See, E. Isichei, *A History of the Igbo People*, London, 1976. This is one of the most acclaimed scholarly works on the general history of the Igbo. So also, A.E. Afigbo, (ed.), *Groundwork of Igbo History*, Lagos, 1992. In this groundwork, prominent historians carried out an in depth research of the history of the Igbo. See also, V. C. Uchendu, *The Igbo of Southeast Nigeria*, Fort Worth, 1965. Compare too with, D. C. Ohadike, *Anioma. A Social History of the Western Igbo People*, Ohio, 1994. On the Igbo (Biafra) war civil war experiences with Nigeria. See, A. A. Madiebo, *The Nigerian Revolution and the Biafran War*, Enugu, 1980. On the aspect of the Christianity and Catholicism in Igboland, See, R. A, Ozigboh, *Igbo Catholicism: The Onitsha Connection 1967–1984*, Onitsha, 1985. See also, V. A. Nwosu, *The Laity and The Growth of Catholic Church In Nigeria: The Onitsha Story 1903–1983*, Onitsha, 1990. See also, Celestine A. OBI, (ed.), *A Hundred Years of the Catholic Church in Eastern Nigeria 1885–1985*, Onitsha, 1985. This text tells the history of the Catholic over hundred years of existence in the Eastern Nigeria. It was published to mark the first centenary of the Catholic Church in Onitsha Ecclesiastical Province within the former Lower Niger Mission. See on Nigeria's story, Crowder, M., *The Story of Nigeria*, London, 1962. See also, Kukah, M. H. *Democracy and Civil Society in Nigeria*, Ibadan, 1999.

97 See for details, P.C. Okuma, *Towards an African Theology. The Igbo Context in Nigeria*, Brussels, 2002.

Such a contextual theology project is inevitable. Since the Igbo have a narrative[98] to tell and such a narrative should never be considered as insignificant to that of any other people. Otherwise the people atrophy!

---

98 S. Hauerwas, *The Peaceable Kingdom: A Primer in Christian Ethics*. Notre Dame, 1983, p. 28. "Narrative is the characteristic form of our awareness of ourselves as 'historical' beings who must give an account of the purposive relation between temporally discrete realities. Indeed, the ability to provide such an account, to sustain its growth in a living tradition, is the central criterion for identifying a group of people as a community. Community joins us with others to further the growth of a tradition whose manifold storylines are meant to help individual's identity and navigate the path to the good."

Chapter Three: The Igbo Worldview at the Service of a Theology

It is a fact that intense and keen study of 'worldview' has not been taken up by most scholars for a long-time, since the kind of knowledge which the subject is supposed to generate has been taken for granted in the developed World. From the vantage perspective of established civilizations, Western Scholars have concentrated more on specific topics related to their lives – literature, political science, religion, art, science and technology, and so on.[99]

It is paradoxical that philosophy, which is one of the basic thought integrating studies, has declined mainly to logic and epistemology. Worldview studies have tended therefore to be reserved to anthropologists who studied the so-called 'primitive societies.' And looking at such 'primitive societies' emphasis has tended to be placed mainly on the religious elements. The essay in the premier work which gave impetus to the subject, *African Worlds* (1955), leaned heavily on the religious topics in spite of its general definition of "World outlook" as relating to "the intricate interdependence between a traditional pattern of livelihood, an accepted configuration of social relations, and dogmas concerning the nature of the world and the place of men (*and women*) in it."[100]

A recent review of the topic, while advocating for the expansion of the perspective of the subject beyond "the level of the mystical", then goes ahead to define worldview in terms of a "space-time framework for the conduct of social life"(J. P. Kiernan). It would appear among Western Scholars some facet must be principal in a hierarchy of aspects. A thing must be defined in terms of its most prominent tendency. The seemingly democratic principle of letting all aspects operate equally in a people's way of life is not allowed full recognition in this type of understanding.[101]

---

99 "Igbo World View and Contemporary living" in 1984 *Ahiajoku Lecture*, published by Culture Division, Ministry of Information, Culture, Youth and Sports, Owerri, p. 61.
100 *Loc. cit.* Italicized addition mine.
101 *Loc. cit.*

However, for our part this holistic understanding is important for our context here inasmuch as we need to grapple with the totality of the Igbo, since whether we admit it or not, the Igbo bring this (Totality – Worldview – *Weltanschauung*) along or should we say it is the totality of this that is the Igbo, while responding to the demands of the Gospel and witnessing to the resurrection of Christ *ad intra*, inner sacramental life of the Church, and *ad extra*, in concrete existential engagements.

In this regard, it is important to note that all hermeneutics of the Igbo is dependent upon 'tradition,' the latter itself depends on a worldview, a narrative and a way of looking at realities.[102] And so each people's reflection and outlook is relative to a particular time and place. Thus a people's worldview is often determined by the specificity of the people's history and convictions. In this way a people always take with them their worldview and approach *ihedi-ihena-ime*, reality and living on all planes – spiritual and physical, from this background. There is no denying this fact. Denying of this fact only leads to a pretense that most times backfires.

Could the Igbo attempt at negating the reality of their worldview in the name of their new found faith not account to most extent for the reason why times the Igbo in the church on Sunday seem to be a different personality outside the church for the rest of the week? One could still raise more questions within this crisis-situation. Why do the Igbo still would like to cling to visiting the native doctor to find out certain ominous things about the fate of his or her dead relatives and friends? Why do the Igbo still believe in reincarnation at the bottom of his or her heart, in spite of the teachings of the 'Official Church 'to the contrary? Why do the majority still clamour for protection from charms and amulet even after believing in the power of Jesus Christ to save them? Why do most still cling to their "Ozo traditional titles" in secret even after threats of sanctions from the local church? Why would they prefer rather to stick to these titles and abandon their Christian faith? Why would most of the people break the Sunday obligation but stay at home on the traditional '*nso-oru*' day

---

102 A. MacIntyre, *Whose Justice? Which Rationality?* Notre Dame, 1988, pp. 326–69.

(abstinence from working on the land on a special day in honour of 'Ala', the earth-goddess)?[103]

Why would the youths (even some adults) prefer long hours of fellowship with the Catholic charismatic renewal movement (a pious society) rather than staying much longer at the holy Mass? Why the enormous quest even among the clergy for beginning 'healing ministry'? On the part of the people, why is the outstanding hankering for 'healing' and miracles for prosperity? Of course, knowing too that it is against their faith to visit the spiritual homes, they do so in secret, in spite of threats of suspension from their local churches. Why do the Igbo Christians not have answers to most of their public situations – in the Government and Work places from their Christian faith? Often their attitude toward their Christian faith is that of timidity – since, they see their local church 'as the big father with the big stick' rather than the one who has come to 'bring good news to the poor, to heal the contrite of heart' (Luke 4:8), 'to seek and to save what was lost' (Luke 19:10) (LG, no. 8) and to set the downtrodden free. Why the high trend of poverty among the people, in spite of the flamboyance of a few? These concerns and more show that there is a problem somewhere. Did the early Missionaries to Igboland take time to study and learn the people's worldview as Paul tried to learn and evangelize the Athenians starting with their principle of the 'Unknown god' (Acts 17, 22–23)?[104]

Paul knew that any effort to undermine a people's reality, of their tradition and cultural values become a kind of an 'estrangement' and a misleading adventure, since at the end of the day the people go back to question and rediscover their particular tradition no matter how many years this takes. Hence it is safer to carry on the people at all times with their

---

103 Uchendu, *The Igbo of Southeast Nigeria*, pp. 95–96. "The Igbo regard *ala,* the earth-goddess, nearest to them, with the possible exception of their ancestors. *Ala* is an earth-goddess, a great mother. She is the spirit of fertility. She increases of man and the productivity of the land. Without her, life would be impossible for the Igbo, who attach much sentiment to the land. It is out of the respect to the earth-goddess that the Igbo are ideologically opposed to the sale of land."
104 *Loc. cit.*

traditions and values *ab initio*.[105] Paul did. Christ did – he used concrete examples and narratives with which his people were at home – 'traditions' of his people that made the message meaningful and evergreen to his followers.

And not only these persons, in the encyclical dedicated to Africa – *Africae Terrarum* of October 29th, 1967, Paul VI referring to African religious Worldview, says, that African traditional religious expression constitute rather "a spiritual view of life...which considers all living beings and visible nature itself as linked with the world of the invisible and spirit"(Article 4). And central to this, continues the Pope, is the "spiritual view of life, (this) spiritual concept is the most important element ...the idea of God as the life or ultimate cause of all things. This concept, perceived rather the idea of God as the first or ultimate cause of all things. This concept, perceived rather than analyzed, lived rather than reflected on, is expressed in very different ways from culture to culture, but the fact remains that the presence of God permeates African life as the presence of a higher being, personal and mysterious"(Article 5). Consequently Paul VI calls for an exchange of meaning between Christianity and African religious tradition.

This is true to the extent that it is paradoxical that, "without tradition we have no means to ask questions of truth and falsity."[106] On the other hand, this is also problematic. Since given this situation, one may ask how can the tradition and values of a people escape solipsism and avoid complacency? Can a people's tradition and values give a ground for judging alternatively other narratives? What form must this take in order to assure objectivity? Since, a people are always embodied within various limitations – of their history, attachment to concrete objects and relation and of the hermeneutical horizons of a shared way of life (tradition) – all of which point to the extent to which a people owes its status and integrity to contingent factors, relations, and objects.[107] Of course the truth of Christian patrimony, the resurrection of Christ is an objective metanarrative that

---

105 S. Hauerwas, *A Community of Character: Toward a Constructive Christian Social Ethic*, Notre Dame, 1981, p. 4; p. 289 no. 8.
106 *Ibid*, p. 95.
107 E. Katongole, *Beyond Universal Reason. The Relation Between Religion and Ethics in the Work of Stanley Hauerwas*, Notre Dame, 2000, p. 69.

goes beyond contingencies, but the *appropriation* of this metanarrative has led to theologies of which the Igbo theology in context is one. Here then as we argued in the first volume of this book,[108] 'Igbo contextual theology' stands vulnerable in its contingency of use of the Igbo worldview (in the light of the hermeneutical metanarrative of the resurrection of Christ and its implication for this people with all they are in its entirety); but this is rather to be overcome by the fact that it is ever ready for *theological Conversation* with other theologies and other people's narratives, as Paul even ventured into *Conversation* with the Athenians.

An understanding of the Igbo worldview and its reconstruction within a hermeneutico-metanarrative framework is important in this context of our enquiry; towards a proper *appropriation* and integration of the resurrection of Christ in concrete witnessing for Him, and contributing towards humanity and World Order, above all making the faith evergreen in Igboland.

In defining such a worldview, the essential thing is not as such to assert what is peculiar or different but to reveal what is consistent and explanatory about the Igbo. What makes this people cannot be defined in individual units but in a combination of elements. Even if people share many characteristics, as they are bound to do since we are dealing with the common human species, it is in the nature of their combinations that we have their specific identities.

Looking at the Igbo, one is tempted to discard them and some of the practices as ignorant and superstitious; one may consider their actions as the results of wishful misapplications of hope and charlatanism. Often, one's doubts are supported by the naiveté of the belief and practices.[109] But accordingly, one is called upon to make distinctions between results of, "excesses of irrationality within popular behavior. There is no doubt that the so-called magico-religious perspective tends to such excesses which are deplorable; our misapplication of logic, such that what we think is in the area of belief or superstition is really in the field of mechanistic causality only we did not know; and differences between what is acceptable and

---

108 P. C. Okuma, *Towards An African Theology.* p. 20.
109 "Igbo Worldview and Contemporary living" in 1984 Ahiajoku Lecture, p. 62.

what is not on the basis of vision of reality. The mechanistic vision of reality has, on the basis of technological achievements, tended to extend its efficacy to areas that are not accessible to such mechanistic causality in the human, social and religious aspects of life."[110]

It is important for one to open one's eyes and take a keen, unprejudiced[111] look again (*Sapere aude!* in the sense of the deployment of this word by Paul Ricoeur) at the actions and traditions[112] of the Igbo and see whether perhaps there is not a more authentic and homogenous direction from which it can be better understood and be helpful and appropriated to witness to the resurrection of Christ for the local churches, the wider human society and the World Order.

---

110 *Loc. cit.*
111 Anonymous, In *Faith and Culture*, published by the Education Department, United States Catholic Conference, Washington D.C., 1987, p. 53. "Our first task in approaching another people, another culture, another religion, is to take off our shoes, for the place we are approaching is holy. Else we may find ourselves treading on another's dream; and more serious still, we may forget that God was there before our arrival." See also, T. Okere, *African Philosophy. A Historico-Hermeneutical Investigation of the Conditions of its Possibility*, New York, 1983, p. 128. From a more Philosophical perspective, Okere argues that, "For black African...it will mean familiarity and identification with their culture. Such identification will enable them to articulate authentically at that ultimate level of meaning which is properly the philosophical, the peculiar understanding of life and reality, which their culture embodies. It is thus a culture can speak by itself, of itself, and of itself. This self-interpretation which is also a self-assertion, is no doubt the best way to restore self-confidence to a humiliated culture."
112 Katongole, *Op. cit.* p. 175. "...Witness offers no guarantee that contact with the 'stranger' will be successful, let alone peaceful. In fact, given the possibility that such contact may expose the limits of a tradition, or throw that tradition into an epistemological crisis, the 'stranger' is often seen as a threat. And so, contact between traditions has tended to be 'armed' with swords and/or defensive ideological self-justifications. This is clearly true, for example, in the case of a religious Constantinianism, which comes literally armed with an extra ecclesia nulla salus evangelizing mission. But it is equally true of a political and economic modernism which 'arms' itself with an evolutionary social theory whose Geltungslogik transcendentally plots traditions on a lineal superior-inferior scale, thus giving it an arrogant posture and mandate of modernizing inevitability."

One needs to understand this people better and at their best through their worldview.[113] Just like, "in order to affirm the theological claim of creation or the scientific-ontological claim of the "big-bang," one must already in some sense stand within the respective Christian or scientific praxis. The self-involving nature of these claims means that there is no transcendental ground from which one can gain access to them but through initiation into a particular way of life which they engender and regulate."[114] 'Initiation into a particular way of life' is the way to *knowing as knowing (qua tale)* and understanding the Igbo and not through times the prejudicial coverage of some media about this people, their cultures and values.

Be that as it may, in the context of this pursuit here, the Igbo worldview could be understood as an ensemble of the way the Igbo view realities in the world, in the human society, in the inner recesses of their being as persons with other persons. The Igbo worldview can be seen through the Igbo tendency to 'concepts', which influences their perspectives towards life,[115] literature, arts, music and drama and above all language. 'Language is like a bank or museum in which, over the centuries, each ethnic group has deposited all it has built up and accumulated in the way of mental and material tools, memories and resources of imagination. By means of an in-depth and wide ranging study of the language (both infra and supra linguistic),[116] through religious documents, fable and legal customs,

---

113 G. O. Ehusani, *An Afro-Christian Vision. "Ozovehe" Toward A More Humanised World,* Lanham, New York, 1991, (reprinted 1997, Ibadan), p. 203. Ehusani in this study in this book arrived at the conclusion in the fourth chapter of this book that, "African traditional worldview is overtly humanistic."
114 Kantongole, *Op. cit.* p. 165.
115 B. Bujo, "Can Morality be Christian in Africa?" in *African Christian Studies,* Nairobi, March 1988, p. 5. Bujo argues that part and parcel of Africa worldview; the fundamental option of the black African is 'Life'.
116 See, *The Guardian Newspaper,* Lagos, Monday June 17, 2002. "The Nigeria Educational Research and Development Council (NERDC) has translated mathematics texts for the first three years of primary school into Hausa, Igbo and Yoruba languages. Apart from the translation of mathematics texts into the three key local languages, 36 of the already identified

medical and educational prescriptions, instruction in craft and technical skills, it is possible to uncover the entire grid pattern underlying a culture or civilization: how people think, how they behave, their conceptions of love, the hereafter, human destiny, and so on.'[117]

The tendency to put what they have into a brief and symbolic form as possible appears to be a key characteristic of the Igbo expression and artistry, whether it is in song or speech, or in body movement. These form the binocular of penetrating the worldview of the Igbo. There is no doubt that

---

583 languages in the country have had their orthographs developed. However, N154.5 million is needed to develop the remaining 550. Nerdc's Executive Secretary, Prof. Ebele Maduewesi, who disclosed this to the *News Agency of Nigeria (NAN)*, added that apart from the orthography problem, language identification in the remaining 11 states, which had been hampered by the lack of funds, indicated that Adamawa had 100 languages, the highest in the country. According to Maduewesi, the council had embarked on massive development of projects designed to spur the use of languages in the country believing that it was only through proper comprehension of the languages that meaningful progress could be made. At the end of the language survey tour in the year 2001, she disclosed that Nasarawa State was second with 53 languages followed by Niger with 39 languages. The states with low number of languages are Ondo, Ebonyi and Zamfara with two languages each. Bayelsa has six languages and Jigawa, eight. More than N1.46 million, she said, had been spent on the language identification project, requiring about N800, 000 to complete the project. Although not yet published, Maduewesi said that mathematics texts for first three years of primary school had been translated into Hausa, Igbo and Yoruba, saying: "The child should be able to use the local language in mathematics in order to be good in the subject." Also, the core curriculum for primary school Agriculture has been translated into Hausa, Igbo and Yoruba but not published yet because of lack of funds. A phrase book, a handbook that can be used as a guide at the point of entry into Nigeria, she added, has been produced in English, Hausa, Igbo and Yoruba. According to her, the production of bilingual dictionaries in the three major languages had been abandoned five years ago because the council had no fund to continue the project. A textbook on the vocabulary of primary science and mathematics in nine Nigerian languages has been published and a quadrilingual glossary of legislative terms in English, Hausa, Igbo and Yoruba for use in the National Assembly has also been published, she said."

117 A. Pieris, "Toward an Asian Theology of Liberation: Some Religio-cultural Guidelines" in D.J. Elnood (ed.), *Asian Christian Theology: Emerging Themes*, Philadelphia, 1980, p. 70.

this casts light and shadow on the faith of the Igbo today as Christians, as human persons in the human society and will continue to do so in the future.

Paradoxically, the Igbo language[118] is of great importance. "Because human beings are not accidentally culturally mediated, but necessarily so, truth does not come as a correspondence to an independently existing reality or the correspondence of language to an independently existing reality or the correspondence of language to an extra-linguistic world. Rather, truth is an interpretative performance realized through and within the cultural linguistic practice."[119] And it is this fact that takes one into understanding of the complexities of the innermost consciousness of the Igbo – 'the cultural linguistic practice' which becomes an encounter in reality in the expression of their faith and in solidarity with human persons in general.

One may "think it is only partially true to say that religion is an 'experience' of reality and language is its 'expression'; the converse is closer to the truth: Language is the 'experience' of reality and religion is its 'expression'. Religion begins with language. Would it be wrong to say that language is *a theologia incohativa* – an incipient theology?"[120]

We take for instance, the biblical narrative of the Master who summoned his servants and commissioned them over his household (Luke 12, 35–48), the Igbo will read a different meaning into the understanding of God as 'Master'; this is because the Igbo cannot conceive of God in *personal terms* like in the case of some Christian stories. It is always God-for-us, God-with-us all.

For instance, when the Igbo refers to God (Lord) as *Onyenweanyi*, a terminology that could be said to be of missionary era in origin (of the most

---

118 Okuma, *Op. cit.* p. 78. Here I have argued that, "in reality then, in order to get things working in this direction of Igbo theology, the Igbo language needs to be developed more as a necessary tool for theologizing." But key questions must also be raised: Who will develop it? How can it be developed when the language of instructions in Schools in Igboland is English; when most of the people prefer to speak more English than Igbo, even when only Igbo are gathered? *Quid a casu?*
119 Katongole, *Op. cit.* p. 172.
120 Pieris, *Op. cit.* p. 70.

common designation of God among the people {Tshuku} Chukwu[121]), a term, which has been deployed wrongly to translate the English word, 'Lord,' he is not referring to God as Master (Lord) essentially in 'Master-Slave relationship' – although this kind of relation exists among the Igbo, as between the boss (*Nnam-ukwu*) and his employee (Odibo). They are instead going beyond the master-slave relationship into making an in-depth and meaningful acknowledgment of God as '*Owusu*' – 'a provider, on whom the citizens depend,' to deploy the imagery of John Pepper Clark in his poem titled, "*Owusu*".[122]

But "the high god (God) too is conceived of in different roles. In his creative role, he is called *Chineke, Chi-Okike* (*Chi – God; Okike* – that creates).[123] To distinguish him from other minor gods he is called *Chukwu – the great or the high god*. As the creator of everything, he is called *Chukwu Abiama*, while as the pillar that supports the heavens; he is called *Agalaba ji igwe*. The sky is regarded as his place of residence and people invoke his name as *Chi-di-elu* – "God who lives above."[124]

In this case, the Igbo perceive the idea of God not only as a provider or a Being on whom they depend, but also as an 'Overseer' (*Overlooks all from his abode – Onone-enu-ogodoya-na-akpu-na-ana*) in their well-being; an inner conviction that leads to an outward expression of trust and reposition of confidence for their fate and destiny as a people of God and as a people belonging to the human society and the visible universe, *Uwa*.

For the Igbo many aspects of that universe exist on two levels – the natural level, and as spiritual forces, *alusi*. These include the sun, *anyanwu*,

---

121 See, *Journals of the Rev. James Frederick Schoen and Mr. Samuel Crowther*, London, 1842, pp. 50–1. "The word 'Tshuku' – God – is continually heard. Tshuku is supposed to do everything …- Their notions of some of their attributes of the Supreme Being are, in many respects, correct, and their manner of expressing them striking. 'God made everything: He made both White and Black', is continually on their lips. Some of their parables are descriptive of the perfections of God."
122 See, *A selection of African Poetry*.
123 V.C. Uchendu, *The Igbo of Southeast Nigeria*, Forth Worth, Philadelphia, London, Tokyo, 1965, p. 94. "The idea of a creator of all things is focal to Igbo Theology."
124 *Ibid*. p. 95.

the sky, (*'igwe'* – the Igbo believe that the sky is larger than the earth; hence the name *igwe k'ala*).[125]

God[126] is closely linked with sky (*igwe*)[127] and the Sun, (*anyanwu*). They are variously seen as his 'home', his 'messengers' or as metaphors of his attributes.'[128]

The *appropriation* of the *essentials* of Igbo worldview as a stepping stone and as a point of departure in explicating the basis of the faith would try to define and describe a better understanding of the 'person of God,' a better way to the faith for the Igbo and in dealing with fellow humans in today's world that professes justice and egalitarianism[129] for all, although the world's political and economic framework today make this dream a mirage and a mere *flatus vocis* without any *fundamentum in rei*. The signs and realities are there to be seen by those who keenly and honestly endeavor to truly see.

In fact, the Igbo worldview does not end with language as highlighted above, instead it seems paradoxical to say that the people's worldview begins with the language as the 'goggle' of seeing the worldview of the people and ennobling their faith and existential engagement now and in the future.

The one important metaphor and hermeneutics to understanding and appropriating the hermeneutical metanarrative of the resurrection of Christ, therefore, is human life in its dynamism of encounter, in its

---

125 *Ibid*. p. 97.
126 E. Isichei, *A History of the Igbo People*, London, 1976, p. 25. "The missionary naturally concentrated on an aspect of Igbo religion which corresponded closely with his own: the idea of God, eternal, the Creator of all things."
127 Uchendu, *loc. cit*. "In pre-British days, *Igwe* was developed into a big oracle, which had its center at Umunoha in Owerri. It was from Umunoha that neighboring communities bought the right to establish their *igwe* shrines. These shrines were not competitive with but complementary to the all-powerful parent oracle at Umunoha. Like other oracles, the *igwe* of Umunoha also functioned as a final Court of appeal."
128 Isichei, *Loc. cit*.
129 *Ibid*. p. 34. Isichei is of the opinion that, "Igbo society was not of course perfectly egalitarian; no society is. The more prosperous accumulated wives and slaves. As in any society, it helped to have a prosperous father."

unfolding in and building of history. If we are going to discover God, it is in the concreteness of human life through the language as a given about each people; even if sometimes we have to be reminded that, inevitably, we have to put on 'spectacles' (our contexts) to look at that human life.[130]

Appropriation of the Igbo worldview is this 'spectacle' that invites putting on through the Igbo language as a necessary tool for theologizing for the people, since the boundaries of a language are the boundaries of a linguistic community which is also a social community.[131] This is important as much as we recognize the truism as Wittgenstein says, that each language has its own logic and is to be understood in its own light.[132] Rather than giving superseding standing to 'one language,' this would lead to the mangling of perspectives of realities instead of the enrichment of the recesses of the richness of human society and the Church. This is part of the reason why since the Enlightenment period until now theologians have sought to demonstrate that it is necessary that theological language be translated into terms that are meaningful and compelling for those who do not share Christianity's beliefs, and not only those who do not share Christianity's beliefs, and not for the unlettered. This we see clearly in the Church's 'aggiornamento' program that was inaugurated by John XXIII and extemded for the rest of the Second Vatican Council.

We notice that in the light of this pathway, the Council's characteristically 'ecumenical spirit' has achieved this. Thus liturgical celebrations could now be held in the language of each people and the Bible translated into different languages, including most African languages, among which is Igbo language.[133]

But it is not enough that we have the bible in the Igbo language, in addition to its written form, "the Bible should be given free hand to circulate orally, just as it did in its original stage of development. Churches should facilitate and exploit oral tradition through more public readings of the

---

130   J. Haers, "A Risk Observed" in T. Merrigan, (ed.), *Louvain Studies* 21(1996), p. 48.
131   A. MacIntyre, *Whose Justice? Which Rationality?* Notre Dame, 1988, p. 373.
132   L. Wittgenstein, *Philosophical Investigations*. E. Anscombe (trans.), New York, 1953, I: no. 23, pp. 65, 67.
133   See the Igbo Bible, *Baibul Nso (Nhazi Katolik)*, Onitsha, 1999.

Bible, more story telling from the Bible, more memorization of passages and verses, more songs and hymns based on the actual using of the Bible passages, more biblical plays, and naturally more scholarly studies comparing tradition in the Bible and African oral literature,"[134] in the light of the Igbo worldview.

Furthermore, the Igbo worldview in a wider sense includes also those things that are part and parcel of the people and need its appropriation 'to tell a story' to the African, the Igbo Christians – which would also enhance the people's faith for the future and their existential engagement.

These should begin with the appreciation of their general conception of reality. In seeking to understand this framework of thought, one would try to find answers to questions like: what concepts appear to govern practice in the areas of religion, social organization and other areas of living among the Igbo in their traditional setting?[135] Into what categories do the Igbo attribute reality? Have the Igbo been able to decode the traditional setting in which they live in order to tell their story and to understand the story of God in the person of the risen Christ?[136]

For instance, the European traditional understanding of reality is at the background of their Christians (equally 'non-Christians' and nominal Christians) using the symbol of egg and chick to tell their story of the resurrection of Christ, where the egg and chick symbolizes 'a new life,' which makes meaning to the basic European Christian looking at these symbols in their homes, streets, public places and in the churches during Easter. By focusing on this symbols and realities they create spiritual impressions that call for an integration and a realization in concrete.

Paradoxically, it is the worldview of a people like the illustration above that provides the framework for the goals of each people and for the hopes and aspirations for the good life of individual persons. For the Igbo by what way they represent and react to their traditional reality in using them

---

134 J. Mbiti, "The Bible in African Culture," in R. Gibellini, (ed.), *Paths of African Theology*, New York, 1994, p. 30.
135 This aspect we shall discuss in chapter Five with special reference to the understanding of 'sacrifice' in the Igbo society and the appropriation of some of its meaning to tell the deeper metanarrative about the Eucharist and its implications.
136 "Igbo World View and Contemporary living" in *Op. cit.* p. 8.

to express their faith is important for the future of Christianity and its true integration in Igboland.

Furthermore, the worldview of the Igbo has to do with understanding their pattern of experience. This has to do with the things that impinge most on their lives. For instance the concept of *ato*, three, is taken to be very symbolic and significant in living experience. This even goes into a saying among the people, *ihe bia na-ato, oto*. Thus, their forbears and more so now make detailed observations of elements of their experiences as this one and they used this knowledge and lived by it. What significance could this be for the Igbo Christian and their concrete integration of the understanding of the persons of the 'Triune God' (*ato-na-otu*) and the faith in their existential engagements?

The Igbo worldview has a high regard for communal life or living together in harmony. This is almost an expression of the life of the early Christian communities in Acts of the Apostles (Acts 4, 32–35). This Igbo worldview must have inspired the Igbo saying, *egbe bere ugo bere*, 'let the eagle perch and let the kite too.' This is justifiable by the fact that, 'a normal African ...community has a close-knit natural and organized system of life. Everyone knows everyone else and they all share numerous commitments together as one people. They constitute a natural community of life and organization that is stable, profuse and long lasting. The system may vary from being patriarchal where inheritance and many substantive rights are through the male or matriarchal where these are through the female.... The Igbo combined expressed individual autonomy with community law and order that kept the greatest authority, not just in the hands of any king or chief, but in the combined hands of community members too, represented by the village elders. Here is a natural system of combined individual efforts for common good, what T. Okere has called stateless democracy.'[137]

The implication of this for the Igbo is that this inspires action, harmony and human solidarity. This spurs action in concrete in the sense that the achievement of the individual raises the existential status of the community. And in this regard, like the widow in the gospel who gave her widow's

---

137 P. Iroegbu, *Kpim of Personality. Treatise on the Human person*. Owerri, 2000, p. 97. See also, *Ibid*. pp. 98–100.

mite in a synagogue contribution, poor Igbo widows for instance would be ready to bring out their last reserves to contribute to scholarship schemes in the community, irrespective of whose child was going to benefit from the scheme. As long as it was a member of the corporate unit, then it was to the good of all.[138]

This solidarity inspires the action of the Igbo today to contribute to the welfare and growth of the local church, the Universal Church and to the general society of human kind. Of course this sense of 'good of all' and the reality of the Igbo saying – *Ndi Igbo, di ka anyi maara, bu ndi na-adighi azu ahia uru adighi* – quest for achievement is a characterization of the Igbo,[139] do not remove from their 'worldview mentality' that the world is torn between check and balance. It is through this maze of 'a world of wits and paradoxes' similar to the imagery of the biblical Job that the Igbo pursue these goals of life in the church and in the human society.

In one summary, the Igbo world is "a world of moving equilibrium... that is constantly threatened, and sometimes actually disturbed by natural and social calamities"(Uchendu); in another it is seen as "a moral order in which man's well-being or failure could be determined by the inscrutable will of the gods", one therefore in which "human existence, in spite of occasional joys, was perceived as being precarious (Kalu). On the one hand, somebody has suggested that the Igbo see their world as "a universe marked by harmony and unity...a Universe which favors the continuity, augmentation, and full realization of life" (Uzukwu); on the other, another has described the Igbo perception of the world as probabilistic such that life is seen as a journey through a market place in which humanity may be divided into winners and losers. (Chidi Osuagwu)."[140]

As much as 'the worldview' of the Igbo give direction to a hermeneutics, to their character, to their story as a people, however, if as Hauerwas says, "adopting different stories will constitute us into different sorts of

---

138 "Igbo World View and Contemporary living", p. 28.
139 *Ibid.* pp. 47–55. See also, pp. 61–68.
140 *Ibid.* p. 45. See also, P. Schineller, P. *A Handbook on Inculturation*, New York, 1990, p. 79. Schineller sees this 'wits and paradoxes' in terms of "One lives close to life; one lives close to death, and hence gains a deeper appreciation for life."

people",[141] then the truth of a story cannot be separated from the truthfulness embodied within the lives of those it has formed. And so, the one overriding criterion that could be suggested for assessing the truth of the various stories is that the truth of each people's story is finally known by the kind of lives it produces.[142] The story embodied in any given tradition "directs us to observe the lives of those who live it as a crucial indication of the truth of their convictions.... At least part of what it means to call a significant narrative true is how that narrative claims and shapes our lives."[143]

In deed the narrative or the story of the Igbo seen in part through the spectacle of their worldview above is at the background of shaping their lives but would be enhanced and ennobled best when their worldview as a people is appropriated into their new status as a people of God, as part of the redeemed humanity through the hermeneutical metanarratives of Christ's resurrection as the 'story of all stories.' Since the hermeneutical metanarratives of Christ's resurrection is inseparable from the story of humanity and the Igbo are part of this redeemed humanity. And so they need *to appropriate – make their own* that salvation and victory won by Christ for humankind. This historical victory challenges all towards concrete witnessing in every facet of the human society and in the Church today.

This 'story of humanity' so to say, that is embedded within the story of Christ's life, death and resurrection – 'the story of stories,' is not a mimicking of our stories but, it is an ensemble of our stories and so our cause to *true testimonial of witnessing* in concrete by *way of appropriation.*

As much as the Igbo have a worldview, a narrative,[144] but this narrative eschews of solipsism. In as much as, the historical nature of truth makes contact with other tradition and worldviews necessarily hermeneutical.

---

141 S. Hauerwas, *Truthfulness and Tragedy: Further Investigations in Christian Ethics*, Notre Dame, 1977, p. 35.
142 Katongole, *Op. cit.* pp. 131–132.
143 S. Hauerwas, *A Community of Character*, p. 97.
144 See some aspects of these stories as portrayed in the novels, Pita Nwana's novel, *Omenuko*, Chinua Achebe's *Things Fall Apart*. See also, E.Isichei, *A History of the Igbo People*, London, 1976. Also, F.A Arinze, *Sacrifice in Ibo Religion*, Ibadan, 1970. And also, A. A. Madiebo, *The Nigerian Revolution and the Biafran War*, Enugu, 1980.

As hermeneutical, it is a confrontation between historically constituted forms of truths – not as between versions (perspectives) of the same truth – but as an interpretative dialogue which is capable of generating critical attentiveness by which truth is dialectically recognized, revised, or extended.[145]

Be that as it may, the Igbo have to be critical of their narrative, their story. This self-criticism consists in self-reflectiveness, which is not a solipsistic achievement on the part of the Igbo. The Igbo learn to question some of its own traditions, question her whereabouts in the church today and in the future, in the Nigeria society today and in the future, and in the wider human society. Above all, this consists in recognizing before the face of the 'story of all stories' the limitedness of their own story as a people and the need for its reunification and its total submission to the light of the hermeneutics of the 'story of stories' – the hermeneutical metanarrative of the resurrection of Christ.

Furthermore, this self-knowledge so to say, is, in great measure, a gift through the presence of others who are willing to listen to, confirm, or challenge one's story. This is at least one way in which "one tradition might inform another of both its limits and possibilities."[146] For, only then is a tradition able to start looking for innovative ways to improve its story, or for alternative practical possibilities. To be able to go on peacefully, it requires innovative and imaginative readjustment.

Imagination here has to do with the presence of another tradition and story, whose practices, and vocabulary provide 'real' options away from the self-imposed necessities of one's tradition.[147] Such an imaginative readjustment is what the hermeneutical metanarrative of the resurrection of Christ provides and challenges to in *testimonium*, witnessing in concrete,[148] which is the main task of this project of the Igbo theology in context.

---

145 Katongole, *Op. cit.* p. 172.
146 S. Hauerwas, *A Community of Character*, p. 48.
147 Katongole, *Op. cit.* p. 175.
148 P. C. Okuma, *A Call to Authentic Living in Christ: The Challenge of the Third Millennium*, Enugu, 1998, p. 4; "…'Christ-Ian': a follower of Christ, a disciple of Christ, a member of the family of Christ, a soldier of Christ, a witness to Christ – by words and deeds (*Eritis mihi testes* – Luke 24:47)."

The inspiration and hermeneutics from this 'story of stories,' remain the point of departure and highpoint for *communicative relation and Conversation*[149] of God in the plight of humanity, his people, of which the Igbo are part of this redeemed who are challenged by this 'story of stories' to witnessing.

Certainly we may try to show how the biblical story makes sense of human life in a way that no other can; but even this becomes clear only when one is part of the story. In the end, the only answer we have to give to the question is along such lines as these: 'I have been called and commissioned, through no merit of mine, to carry this message, to tell this story, to give this invitation. It is not my story or my invitation. It has no coercive intent. It is an invitation from the one who loved you and gave himself up for you.' That invitation will come with winsomeness if it comes from a community in which the grace of the Redeemer is at work. Whether or not it is accepted is not a matter in our power. To be anxious about it, to fret about it, is a sign of unbelief. The one who invites is in control, not we. Kenneth Cragg has said that an anxious witness is a contradiction of terms.'[150]

Thus the God, who triumphed and cares for His own, equally wants His own to share in this victory, through *testimonium*, witnessing. 'Admittedly, this hermeneutical aspect might be related to the notions of 'dialogue' or 'conversation', we have talked about in this work and in its first volume.

However, from a terminological point of view, 'witness' is preferable to these more fashionable expressions because witness preserves the realization that, while contact with others may sometimes take the form of explicit argument and dialogue, the more primary form of hermeneutical contact is the mere presence of another – which leads to a 'display' of the richness of practices and character made possible by the other's particular

---

149 C. Schwöbel, pro manuscripto, *God as Conversation. Reflections on a Theological Ontology of Communicative Relations*, Leuven, November 7, 2001, p. 2. "Taking the understanding of God as conversation seriously implies that God is eventful, relational, personal, communal and that the divine being is freely communicative being so that the world's being is freely communicated and dependently communicative being."

150 L. Newbigin, *Truth and Authority in Modernity*. (In the series, "Christian Mission and Modern Culture"), Pennsylvania, 1996, pp. 82–83.

story. In other words, the primary hermeneutical challenge is not 'listen' to what the other has to say, but to 'see' who the other is, without attempting to reduce the other to an extension of one's self-understanding."[151]

Paradoxically within a contextual parlance, it entails an appropriation of the victory of the victorious Christ, and it is to this witnessing in concrete that this Igbo theology in context challenges the Igbo in their local churches and human society with their entirety – all that they are as a people. It demands courage, a 'willingness' to stand up and stand out to witness for God in Christ in their local churches, in the human society, as the Prophets and the Apostles did, but this time wearing a 'spectacle', their worldview as a people.

In this way, "prophecy will help us to be a continuing countercultural presence in an increasingly secular world. There is a growing respect for other believers and their faiths and ideologies. The dynamics of prophecy seem to combine the urgency of proclamation with the respect for the other and God active in the other that calls for dialogue."[152] We have to tell and live the story faithfully; the rest is in God's hands. What matters for the Igbo are not that they ought to succeed, but that they remain faithful, so that God should be honoured in their aspirations as a people.

---

151 S. Hauerwas, *After Christendom*, Nashville, 1991, p. 159. See also, Katongole, *Op. cit.* p. 173. "Witness carries an immediate association with this normative aspect of peaceableness in a way that dialogue and conversation do not. Dialogue and conversation may tend to obscure the epistemological preoccupation of witness; dialogue by its association with political compromise, and conversation by the liberal aestheticization of communication. Witness, however, is primarily a reminder that the peaceful presence of others is essential for the very conception of historical truth."

152 M. Amaladoss, "Mission as Prophecy" in J. A. Scherer & S.B. Bevans (eds.) *New Directions in Mission & Evangelization. Theological Foundations*, Vol. 2, New York, 1994, p. 72.

Chapter Four: The Paradox of a Spirituality

Whereas the hermeneutical metanarrative of the resurrection of Christ in its 'communicative relation' with Igbo worldview forms the focus for this Igbo theology – for witnessing in concrete in the Igbo church and society in general. The socio-theological hermeneutics of the Eucharist is its 'foundational spirituality.'

Thus, our aim in this chapter is to anchor the spirituality that would form the basis of the life and fount of this unique Igbo theology in the light of entering into dialogue with other 'theologies' and today's world order with its 'sensibilities and non-sensibilities'.

4.1 The Eucharist And The Hermeneutical Metanarrative Of The Resurrection Of Christ

The unveiling of the socio-theological hermeneutics of the Eucharist in the light of Igbo worldview for the post-modern humankind to grasp will justify the fact of what Igbo theology can contribute to humanity, World Order and enhancing the Christian faith of the Igbo in the church today and in their witnessing in the wider human society. This takes into consideration the happenstance and realities of this age of Postmodernity. Accordingly in the words of David N. Power, a discourse on Postmodernity cannot overlook the "current cultural reality."[153] In this regard Paul Lakeland notes succinctly that, "The so-called post-modern character of our contemporary culture affects the religious tradition and how that tradition can meaningfully address such a post-modern world".[154]

---

153 D. N. Power, *Sacrament: The Language of God's Giving*, New York, 1999, p. 12.
154 P. Lakeland, *PostModernity. Christian Identity in a fragmented age*, Minneapolis, 1997, p.ix. See also, G. De Schrijver, "Sacramentaliteits van Het Bestaan in de Overgang van Premoderniteit naar Moderniteit en PostModerniteit," in J. Lamberts, *Hedendaagse Accenten in de Sacramentologie*, Leuven, 1994, pp. 17–64.

Postmodernity, in the mind of the aforementioned author entertains a kind of 'dialectics,' 'by the interplay between the given and the novel.'[155] The Eucharist so to say is to be placed among the 'given'[156] in Christian religious tradition. Its 'givenness' makes it liable to fall into possible 'disrepute', or even to say that it has fallen to such, like some other religious traditions, because of the 'modern secularism that has its roots in the Renaissance and Enlightenment traditions in which the happiness and welfare of man pre-empted the glory of God as the pivotal concern.'[157] Paradoxically, "Something else is happening in our century. The gods are being reborn. When God is dead, the way is open for the return of the gods of pre-Christian times, the gods of volk, blood, sex, and soil. The Enlightenment desacralised the heavens; now society and nature are becoming the new domains of the sacred."[158]

In this kind of situation in the words of the humanistic existentialists – 'everything seems to be permitted.' How can this situation be redeemed? It calls for a rethinking, a rediscovery of the Christian essential spiritual patrimony, namely, the Eucharist,[159] via socio-theological meaning, and its validity as a base for the Post Modern Spirituality.[160] "First, this means a move away from metaphysical explanations of sacramental action, from

---

155 Lakeland, *Ibid*. p. 1.
156 By this fact we mean that it is part and parcel of the Christian heritage, going back to the early History of Christian tradition. It had always been a meal bringing together and ordering the life of the apostles.
157 D. G. Bloesch, *Crumbling Foundations. Death & Rebirth In An Age of Upheaval*, Michigan, 1984, p. 38.
158 *Loc. cit.*
159 T. Aquinas, *Summa Theologiae*, 111a, q.75, aa.2–5. In this article Thomas argues for the fact of Christ's presence in the Holy Eucharist, this has formed the basis of the Catholic medieval Theology. The author does not intend to go into further dialectics on transubstantiation. This supra forms the backbone of our discussion in this write-up.
160 We work on the basis that as, Karl Barth and Tillich acknowledged that Christianity and her realities have 'worldly dimension'. For, Barth, Jesus Christ, the Son of God, entered into this world of brokenness and despair and identified himself with our afflictions and needs. Yet, these Theologians were opposed to a false this- worldliness that excludes any appeal to transcendence. Cf. D.G. Bloesch, *The Ground of Uncertainty* (Grand Rapids: 1971), pp. 42–50.

explanations that focus on the transcendental human subject, and from confidence in the adequacy of sacramental representations."[161]

The Eucharist – 'the Christian paschal is the celebration of Jesus' passage from this world to his Father; his act of total offering and total praise of God, his act of intercession for the world, crowned by his death and his resurrection. In passing from this world to their divine parents with Jesus, Christians die to sin to live a life in conformity with the will of God, in a kind of "rebirth" by which they have "a new understanding" and become "enlightened beings."'[162]

In Igboland, the image Christians often seize in this regard is that of initiation. It is a rite that brings them across a vital threshold to be born again and opens up to them a "new understanding" of the world and of life. This rite and image has the advantage of connecting them both to Christian tradition and to the current reality of African communities of black Africa" and to the rest of humanity.[163] In this way, the Igbo connects his or her life with the life of the Eucharist vis-à-vis the resurrection of Christ and its hermeneutical implications of witnessing in concrete.

4.2. Looking At The Igbo *Sitz Im Leben:* Celebrations Vis-À-Vis Sacrifice And The Eucharist

In his novel, *Things Fall Apart*, which has its setting on the Igbo background, the novelist, Chinua Achebe creates an imagery of a family that invited guests to a new yam festival meal. In this scene the height of the foo-foo (pounded yam or cassava) was so high that the guests on one side could not see their fellows on the other side of the same table. This depicts in a way the large-heart and hospitality typical of the Igbo when they are celebrating and equally when they invite guests to a celebration, which is always a moment of joy and celebration.

This Igbo manner of celebrations has been integrated into the Eucharist. As Eugene Uzukwu writes, "The same joy marks the celebration of the

---

161 Power, *Op. cit.* p. 16.
162 F. K. Lumbala, "Africans Celebrate Jesus Christ" in R. Gibellini (ed.), *Paths of African Theology*, New York, 1994, p. 82.
163 *Loc. cit.*

Eucharist with fanfare as the *Ofala* festival of Christ (yearly outing of the Chiefs) in some Igbo parishes in Nigeria. Even in a regular Roman-type celebration such as the Chrism Mass in the Awka diocese (1985) and the Enugu diocese (1989) in Nigeria, there was a predictable reaction of the Congregation to the charismatic renewal or healing by prayer hymns such as: Are you a winner? I am a winner in the Lord Jesus! Or Higher, higher, higher, Higher, Jesus, higher, Lower, Lower, Lower, Lower, Satan, Lower! People rose spontaneously to declare themselves winners in the Lord Jesus – to lift high the victorious Jesus and stamp out Satan. The note of the festival is unmistakable! This cannot be celebrated with folded hands, but abundant gestures: song, clapping, and dance!"[164]

But this gesture is not restricted to Eucharist, but it is general mannerism about the Igbo in their communities. And this 'goodnaturedness' is applicable to all celebrations that equally bid all present to some kind of participation – family members, special invited guests, friends, neighbours, and even passersby.

As in the case of 'sacrificial feast', which is part and parcel of the Igbo sacrificial rite? According to Francis Cardinal Arinze, in this instance, it "is not just a social thing like a wedding feast after marriage in church. But it is also an occasion for the worshippers and participants to eat together and feel a union with one another."[165]

---

[164] E. E. Uzukwu, "Inculturation and the Liturgy (Eucharist) in R.Gibellini, (ed.), *Paths of African Theology*, New York, 1994, p. 100. See, Cardinal. F. Arinze, *The Holy Eucharist*, Huntington, 2001, p. 112. "Another beautiful practice is that of Eucharistic processions. The people of God confess their faith in this wonderful mystery by going in procession with Jesus in this Blessed Sacrament. They sing hymns of faith, praise, and love. They spread flowers along decorated streets. They play suitable music. They rejoice and praise God as did King David when bringing the Ark of God into Jerusalem, with this difference: that the Christian community has the Emmanuel himself – God with us." There is no doubt that the Cardinal's Igbo background has informed his thought in this aspect.

[165] F.A. Arinze, *Sacrifice in Ibo Religion*, Ibadan, 1970, p. 102. Arinze argues further that, "What may not easily be apparent or what may be questioned by many, and not without reason, is that the worshippers feel a union with the spirits. Here it is necessary to remember that only the joyful sacrifices are being discussed. Only these have a meal."

A times some celebrations or feasts might be occasions for some kind of reconciliation as in the case of husband and wife fallen out with each other, or reconciliation after inter-town wars or the case of reconciling two or more enemies.[166] Often the meal is aimed at reconciling both parties. This is more so when it has to do with in-depth tradition of the Igbo idea of sacrifice, details about this, is beyond the scope of this endeavor here.[167]

Be that as it may, reconciliation has a central role in Igbo religion and practice long before Christianity popularized it among the people. Thus, one can see an apparent parallel between the Igbo and Christian Eucharist whereby; "The Eucharist is offered also to reconcile people with God, to obtain his mercy, forgiveness, and grace. The blood of Christ pleads more eloquently than that of all the victims offered in the Old Covenant."[168]

In both Igbo traditional religion and Christianity as we see it today, 'when life is sacrificed, when it is given back to God, it is made sacred and harmony is restored. This belief is embodied in the Christian doctrine of atonement. A fresh statement of this belief, which makes use of Igbo ideas of sacrifice and covenants, will enable Igbo religion to make another contribution to the religious development of humankind and enhance the faith of the Igbo Christians. Here again, by analyzing the theological elements of Christianity and of Igbo worldview and traditional religion, one can indicate areas where Igbo worldview and traditional religion will be supportive of Christian theology and contribute to its restatement in terms of relevance to the Igbo context in concrete creative actions.'[169]

This fact goes further that even in liturgical celebration, which is characterized by 'action that is creative.' As in the case of the Igbo celebrations that can be called creative in Igboland are marked by the active participation of the whole celebrating community. When the intention for the convocation of the assembly is grasped, there is active participation. But, in addition, when the reasons for the convocation are acted out in assembly,

---

166   *Ibid.* p. 103.
167   *Ibid.* pp. 31–61. In this text, he gives a detailed and in-depth study of sacrifice and its implications among the Igbo.
168   Arinze, *The Holy Eucharist*, p. 37.
169   M. A. Oduyoye, "The Value of African Religious Beliefs and Practices for Christian Theology" in K. Appiah-Kubi & S. Torres, *African Theology en route* (eds.), New York, 1979, p. 113.

the celebration becomes a tensive symbol – an environment for the creation and realization of life.[170]

For example, 'the African Eucharistic prayer, like the liturgy of the word, exudes the African environment. The Land, with its valleys and mountains, rivers and lakes, forests and plains filled with animals, joins in the rhythmic praise of the Creator. African Christian Eucharistic communities display and pray for harmony in this universe. The attention drawn to the body in the liturgy portrays a confident acknowledgment of God's gift of life, which is nurtured and made productive. The experience of the power of the word projects the anchoring of the life of the community in the dynamic ancestral memory that is confessed as reaching culmination in the word of God – Jesus the Christ. In the Christian ritual context, it is this prophetic word that transforms the community and generates the power for transforming the world. In African whole Christian liturgical action becomes a gestural display before God of the community confessing its reception of fullness of life in Christ, a community at peace with its ancestral heritage and environment. The African Eucharistic community expresses in a different metaphor the experiences of the same unique salvation in the Christ that is the faith of the Universal Church.'[171]

But in spite of this liturgical exuberance, one needs to question the actual, concrete action and effect of this on the existential life of the Igbo today. When one compares this with the traditional Igbo Religion with its own ritual and sacrificial exuberance one would notice some kind of difference and some effect it made on the Igbo then and the effect of the missionary Christianity makes on the lives today.

In comparism among the Igbo, broken relations are never allowed to go unhealed. Sacrifices are performed and communal meals held to restore normalcy. Sometimes the persons or families involved undergo 'covenant making.' 'This is a process of oath taking that contains a religious element; one always swears by a divinity who thus becomes the chief witness to the transaction. Covenant meals seal reconciliation and purification ceremonies, since one cannot conceivably work to the disadvantage of another

---

170 E. E. Uzukwu, "Inculturation and the Liturgy (Eucharist) in R. Gibellini, (ed.), *Op. cit.* p. 98.
171 *Ibid.* p. 111.

with whom a kola nut has been shared. Why would some people today in Christianity among the Igbo and some other parts of the World, work against their fellows they shared the same Eucharistic meal? We should investigate what makes Igbo traditional oaths and covenants taking within the contest of the meal seem more binding than the Lord's Supper, the Eucharist today.'[172] A rediscovery of this inner reason and meaning could enhance Christianity's patrimony of the Eucharist and spirituality among Igbo Christians today and contribute to the wider ecclesiastical society and World Order.

4.3 From Understanding Of The Inner Meaning Of The Eucharist To Witnessing In Concrete: A Theology Of Witnessing Today

In the Eucharist, life is equally celebrated but beyond the frontiers of 'temporal awashment', to something that is more lasting. This is based on the fact that Christ is being 'celebrated and renacted, and Christ is our life (Jon 5, 40).' Small wonder, that the Eucharist is the *punctum puncti* of the life of the early Church, and every celebration seem to assume the character of celebrating the life in the Eucharist.[173] In the words of the Fathers of Vatican II, "it is the source and summit of our Christian life."[174] Thus, the impact of the Vatican Council II seems to be so much felt in the area of this celebration of this sacrament, more than any other place in the life of the Church, "First in order of immediate impact were the decree on the liturgy and the subsequent series of documents emanating from the Holy See that dealt with it. Every practicing Catholic had to be aware of these changes – changes that he saw taking place with his own eyes and at the

---

172 M. A. Oduyoye, "The Value of African Religious Beliefs and Practices for Christian Theology", *Op. cit.* pp. 112–113.
173 Candidus Of Fulda, "De passione domini", 5; in J.P. Migne, *Patrologia Latina*, 106.68D-69A.
174 *Lumen Gentium*, no. 11. See also, The Constitution on the Liturgy, *Sacrosanctum Concilium*, no. 10, "The Liturgy is the summit toward which the activity of the Church is directed; it is also the fount from which all her power flows."

very heart of what Catholics had learned their lives should center upon, the Eucharist."[175]

This fact of the 'changes' is not unconnected with recognizing the august place of this sacrament in the spirituality of the age following the Renaissance and Enlightenment periods and their concomitant effects on the spirituality of most human persons. Thus, as Theodore Dobson reiterated, "In the celebration of the Holy Eucharist, we bring ourselves, our souls and bodies as living sacrifices to God – consciously."[176] The consequence of this is that there is a 'transformation', in body and Soul, a transformation that goes beyond the person to touching other human persons, one meets; it has, also, the effect of re-kindling life of love and harmony in the society of humankind. Accordingly, John Paul II says that it is, "Bringing people together in fraternal unity, especially the poor. Serving them, sharing with them the bread of the earth and the bread of love. Building up with them a just world, preparing a new world for the future."[177]

Whereas, every other human celebration may tend to achieve this fact 'temporally,' the Eucharist upholds this permanently.[178] A better understanding of the Eucharist will enhance the above fact, to the post-modern mind; since, "one of the principal tasks facing contemporary theology, lies in transposing the theoretical doctrines of faith into practical imperatives so that, the theological as such will become a principle of action."[179]

---

175 J.O'malley, "Vatican II: Historical Perspectives on Its Uniqueness and Interpretation." In L. Richard, O.M.I, (Ed.), et.al. *Vatican II. The Unfinished Agenda. A look to the Future*, New York, 1987, p. 24.
176 T. Dobson, *How the Eucharist Can Transform Your Life*, New York, 1993, p. 8.
177 *L'Osservatore Romano*, (English Edition), February 26, 1979, p. 9. See, N. Sagovsky, "The Eucharist and the Practice of Justice" in E. D. Reed (ed.), *Studies in Christian Ethics (Liturgy and Ethics)*, Edinburgh and New York, 2002, pp. 75–96.
178 Lanfranc Of Bec, "De corpore et sanguine Christi," in J.A. Giles (Ed.), *Beati Lanfranci archiepiscopi Cantrarensis opera*, in Vol. 2, Oxford, 1844, p. 167. Here, he speaks on the mystery of the Sacraments, and it is within this ambient that the transforming effect of the Eucharist is to be understood.
179 W. V. Dych, S.J, "Karl Rahner's Theology of Eucharist," in P. Rossi, (ed.), et al. *Philosophy and Theology*, Vol. 11, no. 1(1998), p. 139.

This challenging task of theology today is to give expression to a particular belief in such a way that it is seen not as just one more thing that "has to be believed" along with so many others, but rather introduces the believer more deeply into the faith.[180] Consequently it behooves to say that, according to the logic of meaning, 'the Christian meaning and understanding of the Eucharist goes back to the Hebrew notion of "blessing" as the praise of God which recalls his *magnalia*.'[181]

In this regard, "thanks always presuppose a gracious gift[182] which is in fact only real through the thanksgiving, where alone the gift is effective and present. Thus, the Eucharist is the actualizing of the salvific reality "Jesus," through the words of thanksgiving uttered over the bread and wine."[183]

This symbolic act is not unconnected with the fitness of food to express the self-surrender of an 'offerer,' the giving of himself for others, and his fellowship with them.[184] Thus, the German expression, *Eucharistie – Gabe der Liebe*,[185] is applicable here. The implication of this analogy is that the gift[186] has its measure in the giving person of Christ (Eph 4.7).[187] And this

---

180 *Op. cit.*, p. 127.
181 K. Rahner, (eds.), et al. *Sacramantum Mundi. An Enclopaedia of Theology*, Vol. 2, Basle- Montreal, p. 257.
182 D. N. Power, *Op. cit.* p. 276. "The metaphor of gift...express what is given and done in sacramental worship...it "gathers and scatters" all reflections on sacraments by designating sacramental dispensation as an economy of gift".
183 Rahner, *Loc. cit.*
184 *Op. cit.*, p. 263.
185 NB: In 1988, the work of Hans Urs Von Balthasar was published by the Arcdiocese of Freiburg under the above title, meaning in English: 'Gift of Love'.
186 Power, *Op. cit.* p. 277. "The use of the word gift is so marked by its use in human orders of friendship and society that it is not easy to grasp the meaning of what scripture and sacrament say of divine gift. So burdened is gift-giving with impositions on others and so bound is it to certain expectations from the receiver that some recent writers have questioned the possibility of true giving and see it more as the "impossible" to which we may aspire in aspiring to the good and to openness to the other." In the context of sacrament, we can fail to do justice to the superabundance of divine gift unless we are quite careful in using this analogy."
187 P. Casarella, "Analogia Donationis: Hans Urs von Balthasar on the Eucharist," in P. Rossi, (eds.), et al. *Op. cit.*, p. 148.

act of giving is encapsulated in love. It is as it where, an outward manifestation of an inward gratitude – which has love as its zenith.

Consequently, whether we call this august meal: the Holy Communion, the Real Presence, the Lord's Supper, Holy Mass, or Sacrificial meal etc., the Eucharist, is not merely a ceremony of thanksgiving and love; it is also a celebration of love – that heals and transforms the Christian life. It is the sacrament of the covenant, pure gift of love for the reconciliation of all humanity.[188]

We cannot do without eating and drinking together in the Eucharist. In this communing together, the Eucharist forms the fulcrum of uniting Christians with one another and the world in general. Since real love is *contagious*. This solidarity gives rise to an involvement to love and care for one another and for 'common humanity,' that gives rise to what the *Parliament of the World's Religions*, in their *Declaration Toward a Global Ethic* referred to as, a fundamental demand: "Every human being must be treated humanely."[189]

In the Eucharist, by the consecration of the bread and wine, 'we consecrate the social relationships and processes of production which make bread and wine (and other fruits of human labor which they symbolize) possible and available. This way of offering – to Christ (the true bread from heaven) the bread from the earth, that he may bless it and bless all that make it available, and the entire humanity is unique. Since this, leads to an honest 'indirect' acceptance to unite what we have for the rich, poor and the needy. We make a pledge of purpose for collaboration in humanity, instead of monopoly and profiteering; and thus seal the bond of acting 'humanely,' the basis of social justice, and authentic spirituality.'[190] This is *au courant* with the words of G.A. Maloney, that "the true test of how Christian we are is the degree of our involvement in bringing mercy and love to those suffering. "For I was hungry and you gave me food to

---

188 "The Mother of the Redeemer," U.S.A., Catholic Bishops Conference, no. 44.
189 Parliament Of The World's Religions, *Declaration Toward a Global Ethic*, Chicago, 4 September 1993, p. 6.
190 E.'D Igboanusi, C.M.F, "The Eucharist as a basis for Social Justice," in *Encounter. A Journal of African Life and Religion*, Vol. 3, Rome, 1994, pp. 67–68.

eat."(Mt.25: 35–41). We need to hear the anguished cry for justice and human dignity rising from our suffering brothers and sisters and make their burdens our own. What affects others must affect us deeply, since when one person suffers, Christ and all of us suffer."[191]

This inner-meaning and 'radical' logic of understanding of the Eucharist needs an attitude and a disposition in order to be internalized as a way of life.

According to the Parliament of the World's Religion in *Declaration toward a Global Ethic*, "historical experience demonstrates the following: Earth cannot be changed for the better unless we achieve a transformation in the consciousness of individuals and public life. The possibilities for transformation have already been glimpsed in areas such as war and peace, economy, and ecology, where in recent decades fundamental changes have taken place. This transformation must also be achieved in the area of ethics and values."[192] This disposition for transformation is a fact in the affairs of humankind.

> This is to be understood in a way as a 'condition of weakness,' without being weak: it is strength in weakness. It is a disposition that allows to be filled.[193] It is, 'this manifestation of human life and human history transformed by the power of the Spirit that constitutes the 'liturgy of the world.' Whereas, it looks like an impoverishment and a tragedy, that the Spirit is confined within a circumscribed, narrow enclave of the secular with no roots, yet there is something transcendental in the disposition for this transformation in the Eucharist.[194]

This 'disposition of weakness,' allows for the feel of the human condition. It allows for a struggle for humanity. It heals the darkness and the anguish, which call out for salvation – this weakness then, provides the arena in which the transforming power of the Eucharist is felt – because I feel for my brethren (2 Cor.12: 9–10).

In this regard, Mary Oduyoye raises very important challenges to Igbo theology. She writes, "Can African Christians contribute new

---

191 G. A. Maloney, *Mysticism and The new Age; Christic Consciousness in the new Creation*, New York, 1991, p. 184.
192 Parliament of the World's Religion Chicago, *Op. cit.*, 4 September 1993, pp. 13–14.
193 Paul's letter to the Philippians 2:1–10ff. (The New Jerusalem Bible).
194 Dych, *Op. cit.*, pp. 141–142.

symbols and myths for promoting justice and reconciliation? Can covenant meals, symbols of sharing and of acceptance of communal responsibility, begin to happen more meaningfully in the Church? Can more people "break bread together" not only on their knees but in their homes, sharing in the utilization of natural resources?"[195] The rediscovery of socio-theological meaning of the Eucharist via Igbo worldview of communal spirit and sense of hospitality can help to broker these impasses in today's world.

For the traditional Igbo, humanity is first and foremost the *community*.[196] In the first place is the extended family based on blood kinship or on affinity through marriage, and then the clan, the tribe, or the nation.[197] The community solidarity tends also to create requirements of sharing and redistribution of resources, almost in the manner of that of the early Christians in the Acts of the Apostles, so that no individual accumulates and hoards resources that become unavailable to others when they need them. Hence the fear of anyone who surpasses others too obviously in wealth, power or influence. The underlying fear is that such a person becomes a public danger and is likely to use their surplus for selfish purposes over against the others. Only those whose role is that of centres of redistribution (such as heads of families) have surpluses of any kind. Any breach of this requirement of basic "equalitarianism"[198] creates jealousies and ill feelings.[199] This could be comparable to the case

---

195 M. A. Oduyoye, "The Value of African Religious Beliefs and Practices for Christian Theology" in K. Appiah-Kubi & S. Torres, *African Theology en route* (eds.), New York, 1979, p. 111.
196 Of course this does not mean 'communism' but *communalism*. Neither does it mean *Statism* or *State absolutism*.
197 P.A. Kalilombe, "Spirituality in the African Perspective" in R. Gibellini, *Op. cit.* p. 122.
198 V. C. Uchendu, *The Igbo of Southeast Nigeria*, p. 19. "The Igbo world is based on an equalitarian principle. Equality or near equality ensures that no one person or group of persons acquires too much control over the life of others.... What the Igbo mean by an equalitarian society is that which gives to all its citizens an equal opportunity to achieve success. The stress is on achievement. They recognize that "a child who washes his hands clean deserves to eat with his elders."
199 P.A. Kalilombe, *Loc. cit.*

of the distribution of needs in the apostolic Church in the Acts of the Apostles that necessitated the appointment of the seven deacons (Acts 6, 1–7). This keynote solidarity among the Igbo is extended in a special way to strangers.

In this regard, with an appropriation of this Igbo worldview to the Eucharist, which is the fulcrum of Christian worship, throws perhaps the greatest challenge to human solidarity with the divine and fellow human beings, in the world today. This fact is analogous to Karl Rahner's description of the Eucharist as including not only a "spiritual movement of the sacramental event outwards to take effect in the 'world,'" (the descending movement), but also an ascending "spiritual movement leading from the world to the sacrament,"[200] although, this unique analogy of Karl Rahner embody both the offer and the acceptance of grace.[201]

In the light of theology, which aims at transposing the theoretical doctrines of faith into practical imperatives so that "the theological as such will become a principle of action,"[202] and hope for humanity becomes the prospect of theological investigations. So that, 'the need to release our own living images of God's love for humanity back to God becomes a reality, more so that we may be incorporated into the Son's *Eucharist* to the Father.'[203] This essential turning point is a way toward grasping the socio-theological dimensions of the Eucharist; more so as a key way for living the Igbo to live the gospel by the way of witnessing in today's world.

Dorothy Day in her autobiography seemed to have captured this point well: "We want, rather unreasonably, sensible feelings of love. St. Teresa says that the only way we can measure the love we have for God, is the

---

200 K. Rahner, "Considerations on the Active Role of the Person in the Sacramental Event," in *Theological Investigations*, Vol. 14, Baltimore, Helicon and New York 1976, p. 162.
201 Dych, *Op. cit.*, p. 129.
202 *Ibid.* p. 139. See also, L. Leijssen, "Current Theology. Sacramental Theology: A Review of Literature", In *Theological Studies*, 55(1994), p. 661. "... Sacramental theology has retrieved the importance of rooting its thought in actual celebration rather than in abstract concepts."
203 Casarella, *Op. cit.* p. 175.

love we have for our fellows...and if you and I love our faulty fellow-human beings, how much more must God love us all."[204]

In this way, 'the Eucharist records a vertical and horizontal dimension. Vertically, it is both a sacrament and a symbol of God's union with humanity. And horizontally, the Eucharist is a sacrament and a symbol of the human being 'born' to humanity's unity with his or her neighbors.'[205]

If the Eucharist is grasped this way, that is, in the light of the dialogic and interpersonal nature of all sacramental activity, it helps to remove any hint of the magical or mechanical understanding of sacramental efficacy of which the church has been accused.[206] This 'demystification,' will concretely lead to a spiritual praxis. In this way, the faithful re-enacts the one sacrifice of Jesus Christ, not only in the sacramental meal, but their activity also receive that stamp from the salvific deed of Christ, consequently, the faithful now, does not celebrate the Eucharist principally as the *anamnesis*,[207] as that which borders 'on mere words of worship,' but also on concrete everyday life existential engagement.[208]

Thus, this fact enhances and compliments the issue that the Eucharistic gift stands not only for the giver and its acceptance by God, but also of the fact that there is a self-communication of God to the person offering the Eucharistic gift. This communion transpires as it where to the persons, the Christian meets in the world.[209] Thus, 'the somatic real presence of Jesus makes possible the deepest confrontation of Christ with Christians and the 'Communion.'[210]

In this regard, John Paul II observes that the Eucharist brings about a New World, marked by filial relations with God and fraternal relations

---

204 Union Square to Rome, 162.
205 G. O. Ehusani, *A Prophetic Church*, Ibadan, 1996, p. 41.
206 Dych, *Op. cit.*, p. 129.
207 Anamnesis, here means: 'not only the subjective presence in the consciousness of the participants, but the objective presence, in actual reality in the acts and words.' Cf. K. Rahner, S.J, et. al. *Sacramentum Mundi, Op. cit.*, Vol. 2, p. 266.
208 J. Verstraeten, pro manuscripto, *The Rediscovery of Meaning in Professional life: Perspectives for a Spirituality of the Laity in the Twenty-First Century*, Leuven, 1999, p. 1.
209 Rahner, *Op. cit.*, p. 265.
210 *Loc. cit.*

with people, "bringing people together in fraternal unity, especially the poor. Serving them, sharing with them the bread of the earth and the bread of love. Building up with them a more just world, preparing a New World for the future."[211]

What is the world without love, and what is love without God? But, God is not 'out there,' as the King, who has enclosed himself in a hidden castle, removed from the human reality. Contemporary Christology affirms that *the transcendent* is truly in our midst. God is not to be limited to a spiritual realm, but is fully present to all historical reality.[212] Consequently, the reality of the 'symbolized' really becomes present in the human society.

Through the Eucharist – 'the symbolic presence,'[213] the reality of the symbolized – of love for persons, self-sacrificing for humanity, healing of broken relationships, transformation of the world, improving the situation of those suffering from the effects of evil, and setting indebted countries free, are known in the medium of 'Symbol,'[214] of the Personality of God as Word, but also simultaneously unknown.[215] Consequently, in the Christian the reality of the Eucharist is to be known through acts that depicts those of the 'Personality of God as Word.' Therefore, "the Eucharistic worship can only be *authentic* if it makes us grow in the awareness of the dignity of every person and particularly sensitive to all human suffering and misery, to all injustices and wrongs, and seek the way to redress them effectively."[216] Herein, the proposal of Hans Küng for an *ethic of responsibility*[217] for the world becomes a priority of affection for a Christian:

---

211 L'osservatore Romano, (English Edition), February 26, 1979, p. 9.
212 L. Richard, "The Mission of the Church: A Contemporary Agenda" in L. Richard, O.M.I, (eds.), et al. *Vatican II: The Unfinished Agenda*, New York / Mahwah, 1987, p. 66.
213 Dynch, *Op. cit.* p. 130.
214 Karl Rahner conceives the humanity of Jesus as this symbol, which also refers to as the grammar of God's self-expression outward into creation. (Cf. Rahner, *Op. cit.* 1978, p. 223).
215 Dynch, *Loc. cit.* This view seems similar to the Heideggerian connotation of 'presencing of Sein.'
216 Ehusani, *Op. cit.* p. 41.
217 See, H. Küng, *Yes To A Global Ethic*, London, 1996.

'It presupposes a conviction.'[218] Not only to answer to one but in love to answer for all.[219]

The Eucharist obliges the Christian to care for humanity and to take responsibility, because the Word of God did. It obliges the Christian to the bond of the most intimate unity of man with God and of men with each other, through Christ.[220]

In work for instance, it obliges participants to work for and promote the "bread" which every man and woman needs. This "bread" without which the human person dies consists of nourishment, work, dignity, liberty, love, and respect for everyone's culture. It seems hypocritical, to share and commune with Christ our brothers and sisters in the Eucharist without sharing and communing with our brothers and sister in the sanctuary of the universe.

In this regard the "sacramental ritual is one that brings with it the face-to-face encounter and the hand-to-hand communion which signifies the order of divine justice to which the testimony of Jesus speaks and that of the spirit prompts."[221] In this vein, the breaking bread around the altar commits us at the same time to the breaking of earthly bread with our brothers and sisters in the highways and by ways of life.[222]

The essence of this fact for the Igbo theological foundation and indeed, for the Igbo of the 21st century is that – the Eucharist becomes not 'a mere symbolic attitude on the altar of the sacrificial meal,' but a form of spirituality that is to be embedded into real life. In this way, the spiritual cannot be reduced to internal-church community life alone, but must go beyond to become fruitful for the world according to the 'logic of Christian witnessing'. This requires the cultivation of *an incarnated spirituality*.

---

218 H. Küng, "Global Politics and Global Ethic," *Unpublished Lecture*, Brussels, March 9, 2000, p. 2/2.
219 Power, *Op. cit.* p. 300. "The analogy of justice must therefore complement the analogy of testimony. Distributive justice is an ordering that allows each and all their rights and their needs for a dignified human existence. It has its quid pro quo."
220 Rahner, (eds.), et al. *Sacramentum Mundi*, Vol. 2, p. 266.
221 Power, *Loc. cit.*
222 D. Lane, "The Eucharist and Social Justice, "in *The Eucharist and Unity*, Catholic Bishops' Conference of Nigeria, 1992, p. 27.

This includes 'the reintegration of faith and participation in the development of the world.' Such a reintegration requires, "a rediscovery of the mystical experience of the real world as *milieu divin*, as a reality on its way to the fulfillment of its human and spiritual potential".[223]

The grasp of this 'other-worldly' attitude and a discovery of this meaning in the Eucharist will bring a change of the Christian attitude toward the world, toward life and human persons. Since as it where, "Attitude is an important criterion and cause of religiousness, though it is commonly mishandled in religious reflection by (1) skewing the anthropologically central variable of attitude toward "feeling," on the side of affect, or toward "disposition," on the side of will, and (2) obscuring different basic forms and validities of religious attitude by insisting on one overly narrow or misleadingly rounded-out conception of devoutness (most often, "faith")."[224] The implication of this fact is that the Eucharist should ignite 'dual dimensional attitude,' that should in fact be seen as 'one-type-spirituality': love and concrete, creative action, the absence of these the Eucharist can be a sacrilege,[225] and theology mere *flatus vocis* without any *fundamentum in rei*.

In this regard, 'Christians should not marginalize themselves in society. They should not construct modern catacombs and hide in them. They should not allow angry demonstrators, supporters of political factions, and sports fans to have the monopoly.... They should not hesitate to get up and be counted for Christ. The Eucharist therefore is of continuing relevance among peoples and cultures around the world,'[226] especially for the Igbo as a spiritual foundation for this challenge to witnessing.

---

223   J. Verstraeten, *Op. cit.*, p. 11.
224   S. G. Smith, "Three Religious Attitude" in P. Rossi, (eds.), *Philosophy and Theology,* Vol. 11, no. 1, p. 3.
225   T. Balasuriya, *The Eucharist and Human liberation*, London, 1979, p. 171.
226   Cardinal. F. Arinze, *The Holy Eucharist*, p. 113–114.

Chapter Five: A Theology at the Service of the People: Igbo Situations and the World Order

'Theology' worth the name today must be relevant to the concrete situation of the people. In as much as the victory of the Risen Christ salvaged the whole human person, *totally and adequately considered*. Such a theology would *ipso facto* eschew the 'Great Fallacy'- "that the body was evil and the soul good, that time was corrupt and eternity pure, that earth was to be shunned and heaven sought, that flesh was the seat of impurity and spirit the seat of blessedness."[227]

Apart from the fact that this separation are not only awkward, inaccurate and unhelpful but that they are, in almost all cases, just plain wrong. They do not add meaning to our lives or give us good interpretive tools; on the contrary they distort our lives and lead us to faulty understandings of who we are as "people of God," and equally part and parcel of humanity – what the world is like.[228]

In the same vein, it tends to render the concrete implication and relevance of this hermeneutical metanarrative of the resurrection of Christ to human conditions and situations inappropriate. Which is not plausible. Be it as it may, part of the concrete relevance of the appropriation of this 'story of stories' – the resurrection of Christ is to tell our own stories. Since the human conditions – community stories are embedded in this story of stories, which as it where encompasses the entirety of humanity stories.

---

227 R. M. Brown, *Spirituality and Liberation*, Philadelphia, 1988, p. 27. "The Great Fallacy has been around a long time, despite the fact that Judaism, out of which Christianity grew, was never seduced by it. On the contrary Judaism has always had a positive view of the importance and sacredness of the created order and all who inhabit it. Indeed one of the most robust resources for Christianity in combating the Great Fallacy is deeper immersion in its Jewish roots."
228 *Ibid.* p. 26.

This is *au courant* with the fact that, "we learn to describe through appropriating the narratives of the communities in which we find ourselves"[229] since we are part and parcel of our communities in which we find ourselves and in wider sense part and parcel of the community of humanity and so we cannot theologize today as if we are coming from a different abode into the human condition or people's concrete situation.

In the light of our project here, hermeneutics of this metanarrative is thus emancipatory and empowering in the light of the victory of the Risen Lord that sets his people free from all entanglement and restores hope and prospects for the Igbo church and people.

While women play conspicuous roles in the life of the Igbo society and the church, this role is to be enhanced towards the challenges of witnessing facing the Igbo society and the church today.

Equally within this ambient, the media, political and economic situation of today vis-à-vis migration and globalization cannot escape this panoramic discussion too, because of their influence in the general lives of all peoples today. Especially as we begin to see that these themes cannot be considered as irrelevant to theological discourse and concrete witnessing as they have influences on the lives of peoples in the church and society – the Igbo society is not left in these contemporary challenges towards enhancing the life they live now and the one they want to live in the future.

5.1 Enhancing Igbo Womebn For The Society And The Church: The Challengee Of Today's Witnessing

"We are on the same parlance with household properties," cries Mrs. Mperesoe, "what can we do, this is our predicament?" She added. This paradoxical pathetic and heart-palpitating outburst of Mrs. Mperesoe sums up the age-long situation allegation made against the plight of women in African as suggested and argued by some bias authors about African women – that they are exploited?

---

229 S. Hauwerwas, *The Peaceable Kingdom: A Primer in Christian Ethics*, Notre Dame, 1983, p. 42.

According to the proponents of this biased position, the female child is counted as 'nothing' in Africa; she was not given any formal education, but only recently. Of course this writer believes that this has nothing to do with the maginalisation or discrimination of women in African, but in particular in Igboland; but it has more to do with poverty in the families that often place restrain on children (male and female) going to school, contrary to what some African writers had suggested.

Some of these biased writers continue to make their case that the African woman had only to engage in the home informal education of learning how to cook from the mother and attending to house chores, until suitors arrive to take her away, the father of the house uses the dowry to carter as such for the male-child's future. She goes away to continue the same housemaid life in the husband's house. Of course, she is not entitled to any inheritance from both parents when they die. But this argument would be found wanting in the situation of the Igbo girl-child, who had as much future and prospect as their male counterpart.[230]

These biased proponents of discrimination of women in Africa will continue to argue that this fact is not unconnected with an age-long tradition and cultural prejudice against the girl-child in African society and cult. Whereby the base their argument on the fact that "Certain people, however, are occasionally excluded from participation.... Women are generally excluded from the inner parts of shrines. It is their work to clean up the place of worship and convey the victim, food and wine to the place of sacrifice."[231] Even it was considered abominable and even an affronted for a woman to climb palm tree.[232]

Of course all these are not seen in Igboland as discrimination or maginalisation of women as such, even among the women themselves, but the fact is that in Igbo society and traditional set-up, which might not be the same for all African peoples, there is division of labour.[233] Men have their

---

230 See, C.O. Acholonu, *Motherism. The Afrocentric Alternative to Feminism*, Owerri, 1995.
231 F. A. Arinze, *Op. cit.* p. 23. He added that in an occasion as cultic worship, that women "in their periods are not to take any part in this."
232 *Ibid.* p. 30.
233 Acholonu, *Op. cit.* p. 43. "I do not know any African society in which there is no division of labour in agricultural production and economic activities of

duties and women have theirs too.[234] There are no usurpations. Even in the case of traditional religion, women have often assumed the position of 'priestesses'.

Even today some African writers who still look through the binocular of the Western world still raise alarm of the appalling situation of girl-child, women in Africa society. For instance, Bernadette Mbuy Beya in a special interview she granted to *Publik-Forum, Zeitung Kritischer Christen* (25 January 2002) titled, *Frauen in Afrika. Stoppt die Gewalt* (English: Women in African. Stop the Violence!). She presents the following key cases[235] – here summed up as follow,

➢ That systematically the men destroy the women through prostitution, AIDS and sexual sicknesses.
➢ If a woman cannot get pregnant in Africa, they people say that the woman is guilty but this is not always true medically.
➢ The dowry of the daughter is the income for the family of the man.
➢ The men inflict physical violence on the women and beat them.
➢ When the man is tired with the wife, he can send her away and often the kids stay with their father.
➢ The whole life of the African woman is a bad influence from the man.
➢ When adultery is committed – it is the woman who suffers, whereas the man is exempt in the traditions.

---

the entire family. If men were farmers, women were food processors and traders. Where women and men were engaged in the same productive activity such as farming or weaving, the produced different items. Among the Igbo, females and males grew different crops."
234 See, J.T. Agbasiere, *Women in Igbo Life and Thought*, London, 2000.
235 B. Mbuy Beya, "Stoppt die Gewalt! Afrikanerinnen klagen an: Frauen werden vergewaltigt, unterdruckt und eingeschuchtert – im Namen der christlichen Religion" in *Publik-Forum, Zeitung Kritischer Christen* (25.January 2002), no. 2, pp. 22–24. It is worth noting that the subtitle of this article, "Afrikanerinnen klagen an: Frauen werden vergewaltigt, unterdruckt und eingeschuchtert – im Namen der christlichen Religion" reads in English – "African women say that they are raped and suppressed in the name of Christian Religion." Whether this is true or not is left to our consciences and more so to concrete action of redressing from the situation. Bernadette Mbuy Beya is a feminist theologian from South of Congo, and this her position is totally at variance with that of women in Igboland. No relevance at all.

From this kind of biased standpoint and overgeneralization, it is easier for an outsider to adduce quickly that the entire Africa society is 'male centred' – that would mean to say that the males are the lords of the communities and the families, whereas women only attend to their role as mere housekeepers and 'manufacturers' of children for the man. Yet at the end of the day, women are also expected to work themselves out in the farms – digging, ploughing, and cultivating crops and seedlings – to keep the household going. It is a must they have to do. Whereas men are overseers and king makers in the entire traditional set-up. Propagators of this kind of biased position would conclude.

But the protagonists of this kind of position forget that, "class and caste are two major determinants of status in traditional Africa. Members of the nobility or ruling classes male and female, enjoy a high status while the untouchable slaves (male and female) suffered and still suffer subordination and segregation by the rest of the society. In most traditional African societies, the peasantry suffered exploitation by the wealthy and powerful. Indeed, 'might' was often considered 'right', and in such a situation the weaker was taken advantage of, hence the success of the slave trade. *The crux of the matter, therefore, is that exploitation, subordination and stratification in traditional Africa was not gender (or sex) specific, rather it was class, caste and power-based and has been ever since.*"[236]

One has to add that those African intellectuals and foreigners who argue that women in Africa are 'marginalized and are mere tools in the hands of men' argue from the position of 'vincible ignorance'. As much as it cannot be said to be true of most parts of African, it cannot be held to be the reality on the ground in Igbo society in particular.[237] "The women

---

236 Acholonu, *Op. cit.* p. 51. Italics mine.
237 See, Ifi Amadiume's book, *Male Daughters, Female Husbands*, Zed Books, 1987. In this book the author, 'examines the relationship between sex and gender in pre-colonial, colonial and postcolonial Africa. She argues that in pre-colonial societies, there was gender flexibility, which allowed women and men to share important social roles and status, thus enabling women to achieve power in economic, social and political institutions. Colonialism and European domination imposed a more rigid concept of gender that excluded women from power. However, aspects of traditional African women's organizations have carried over into modern national politics.' See also,

members of an Igbo village are of two categories: the *umuokpu*, who may be unmarried, married, divorced, or widowed women who belong to the village by descent, and the *ndom alu alu* who belong to it by marriage."[238] These two groups of women in Igboland are not subjected to the men. Victor C. Uchendu makes a very important point here, "The African woman regarded as a chattel of her husband, who has made a bride wealth payment on her account, is not an Igbo woman, who enjoys a high socioeconomic and legal status. She can leave her husband at will, abandon him if he becomes a thief, and summon him to a tribunal, where she will get a fair profit as she sees fit."[239]

Women were powerful people in the traditional Igbo society and could not be neglected by their male counterparts. In Igbo society, everybody had his or her own role to play in the entire traditional setup. Women as much as men[240] in some places in Igboland were entitled to family inheritance, a clear case among others is that of *Ohafia* and *Abam* peoples of Igboland among others.[241]

Cardinal Arinze argues that, "Women have much more power than was generally recognized by early authors. They can hold their own not only by means of public demonstrations, group strikes, ridicule and refusal to cook for their husbands, but also by their inherent vitality, courage, self-reliance and uncommon organizational ability."[242]

The strength of women in Igbo society could also be seen in the case of the position of *Umuada* group in the Igbo society in adjudicating matters.

C. O. Acholonu, *Motherism. The Afrocentric Alternative to Feminism*, Owerri, 1995.

238 V. C. Uchendu, *The Igbo of Southeast Nigeria*, Forth Worth, Philadelphia, London, Tokyo, 1965, p. 86.

239 *Ibid.* p. 87. See also, J.T. Agbasiere, *Women in Igbo Life and Thought*, London, 2000.

240 Uchendu, *Ibid.* p. 57. He however argues that, "To have a male child is to strengthen both the social and the economic status, for it is the male child who inherits the father's property."

241 P. Iroegbu, *Kpim of Personality. Treatise on the Human person*. Owerri, 2000, p. 97. "The system may vary from being patriarchal where inheritance and many substantive rights are through the male or matriarchal where these are through the female...."

242 F. A. Arinze, *Sacrifice in Ibo Religion*, Ibadan, 1970, p. 4.

Similar cases are that, "Igbo women (wives) also use the weapon of general domestic boycott to get their husbands or the entire male community, to carry out the wishes of the women in political and social matters. In this way they often made peace between their community and other communities in matters of war and inter-community squabbles. Seen in this light they were actually (and still are) the final arbiters in community politics and local socio-political affairs."[243] A historical case of the strength of women in Igboland is also to be seen in the famous Aba "Women riot," or, as our people choose to call it, the "Women's War" which started in November 1929 against the British rule.[244]

Today in the Igbo church, women are strong forces to reckon with in advancing the welfare of the dioceses, parishes and station-churches. As against the position of some writers like Rose Zoé-Obianga, that, "women have been allowed to give only a spontaneous expression of their faith, one that is naïve and credulous. Their ideas are of no consequence. Their point of view leaves the world indifferent. Their self-awareness seems dangerous because it could dethrone man from his pedestal."[245] Igbo women have been key factors in supporting the faith and organizing welfare projects for their communities, like building churches, rectories, community maternities, and rural road repairs works.

Concretely here, one needs to see clearly – *Sapere aude*, in order to do thorough balancing of judgments on the position of women in African and Igboland in particular. This would help one overcome the rash judgment

---

243   Acholonu, *Op. cit.* p. 47.
244   Uchendu, *Ibid.* p. 5. See also, *Ibid*, p. 47 "In 1928 the adult males were directly taxed for the first time and the Native Treasury was added to the Native Court complex. The following year, Okugo, a warrant chief from Oloko, touched off a massive protest of Igbo women when he attempted to assess their property in his area. The association of taxation with the assessment of wealth was a logical one. Before their taxation in 1928, the property of the men had been assessed in 1927. What other reason could justify the assessment of women's property, the women reasoned, unless a plan to tax them was in the offing? This mishandled protest (called the Aba Riots in Government reports), which left thirty-two women dead dying and thirty-one wounded, dramatically revealed the problems and the weakness of the administrative system."
245   R. Zoé-Obianga, "The Role of Women in Present-day Africa" in Appiah & Torres, *Op. cit.* p. 147.

against African women, often associated with foreigners and African intellectuals who have no in-depth knowledge of their traditional setup.

One of the tasks of this 'contextual Igbo theology' is to help to develop theories to under gird sound pastoral programs and adequate care of this balancing of judgment, more so to enhance the role and place of women in the Igbo society and church towards witnessing adequately with the men co-responsibly[246] for the good of humans in the Igbo society and church and in the Nigeria society in general. Since such "participation of women in the life of the Church and society in the sharing of her gifts is likewise the path necessary for her personal fulfillment – on which so many justly insist today – and the basic contribution of woman to the enrichment of Church communion and the dynamism in the apostolate of the People of God. From this perspective the presence also men, together with women, ought to be considered."[247]

One has to recognize that in the apostolic church[248] in spite of most of the disciplines coming from a Jewish traditional background that

---

246 John Paul II, *Christifideles laici: On the Vocation and the Mission of the Lay Faithful in the Church and in the World*, (Vatican translation), Vatican City, 1987, no. 52, pp. 135–136. "Therefore, the coordinated presence of both men and women is to be pastorally urged so that the participation of the lay faithful in the salvific mission of the Church might be rendered more rich, complete and harmonious." See also, E. E. Uzukwu, *A Listening Church. Autonomy and Communion in African Churches*, New York, 1996, p. 138. "When the synod Fathers of the Special Assembly for Africa were talking about collaborative ministry, they had their eyes on all the laity without distinction. There was great sensitivity to highlight the role of women in introducing a certain quality into the new model of church as family."
247 John Paul II, *Christifideles laici*, no. 51, p. 135.
248 B. J. Machaffie, *Her Story. Women In Christian Tradition*, Philadelphia, 1986, p. 23. This writer is aware of the fact that "Anyone who wishes to study the status of women in the first six centuries of Christian history is faced with a challenging task. During this period the church spread beyond Judaism and Palestine into the vast expanse of Greco-Roman culture. It was both persecuted and elevated to a position of eminence, all the while struggling to come to terms with the intellectual movements of the ancient world. The variations in belief and practice from place to place and century to century are great. At the same time, our sources of information for this phase are scarce and often fragmentary and ambiguous. Yet the early years of Christianity are vital to the status of women, for they established attitudes and practices that still continue in the Christian community."

discriminated against women, yet couples like Prisca and Aquila (see, Acts18, 2; 1Cor.16, 19) in the Acts of the Apostles also administered some conspicuous roles in the church of their day and society. They collaborated in mission.[249] Although the standpoints of this study here has not the controversial question of the ordination of women in view.

However, we were meant to understand that Prisca and Aquila are the only Christian couple of the first century A.D. whom we both know by name and about whose work as a couple among the early Christians we are informed. The woman participated as much as the man without discrimination in the apostolate of the church and society.

We were comparatively informed that both, Prisca and Aquila were among the founders of the first Christian Community at Rome where they were in the year 49 A.D when the Emperor Claudius expelled all the Jews from Rome. Acts 18:24–26 tells about their great teaching authority. When the Alexandrine missionary Apollos who is characterized as eloquent and well versed in the Scriptures preached at Ephesus, Prisca and Aquila together "took him aside and explained the Way of God to him more accurately."

In all these activities Prisca and Aquila played an important part as Paul's special friends and core members of his small Christian community. Paul even confesses in Romans 16:4 that they "risked their necks for my life." One peculiar thing is the fact that wherever, Prisca and Aquila are mentioned in the New Testament, they are mentioned together. They moved together from Rome to Corinth, on to Ephesus and back to Rome. Together they take on the sensitive task of correcting the theology of a prominent Christian preacher of their time, together they risk their necks for Paul, together they host the church that meets at their house.[250]

---

249 See, E. E. Uzukwu, *A Listening Church. Autonomy and Communion in African Churches,* New York, 1996, p. 138. "When the synod Fathers of the Special Assembly for Africa were talking about collaborative ministry, they had their eyes on all the laity without distinction. There was great sensitivity to highlight the role of women in introducing a certain quality into the new model of church as family."

250 R. Bieringer, "Death and Resurrection of Christ. Effects on all" in Notes on Pauline interaction with the Corinthians, (part III, V), *Leuven Lecture notes,* 2001.

Furthermore, Vatican II Council recognizes and eschews dichotomy in apostolate of witnessing in the Church and Society of today – especially in its *apostolicam actuositatem*, the decree on the apostolate of the laity. They Council used the word, 'laity' to refer to both men and women in the apostolate of the Church; so that whatever is said of men is equally addressed to women too.[251]

In this regard, the norm of equality[252] likewise rejects all double standard sexual morals, which discriminate against certain persons or groups to the advantage of others on the basis of an alleged "difference of values", whether or not it is legitimatised metaphysically, social-scientifically, or socially.

It is paradoxical that "through ages of socialization the majority of women accept the subsidiary and complementary roles reserved to them in African culture and the Christian church. Our proposal of the ministry "with large ears" or leadership in the service of listening, which recognizes the initiative of the Spirit of Jesus in the church and which pays close attention to the conversations at all levels of the People of God, may lead to stronger leadership roles for women within the African church, upset human/cultural forecasts, and rejuvenate the church-community."[253]

Thus Igbo theology in context would take care of balancing seemingly imbalances in Igbo church and society today among men and women,[254]

---

251 See, "*Apostolicam Actuositatem*, Decree on the Apostolate of the Laity," November 8, 1965, in *Decretum De Apostolatu Laicorum*, Romae, Typis Polyglottis Vaticanis, 1965. For a good English translation of this Decree of Vatican II, see, N. P. Tanner, S.J., (ed.) *Decrees of the Ecumenical Councils, Vol. II (Trent to Vatican II)*, London, 1990. See also, Uzukwu, *A Listening Church, Loc. cit.*

252 Uchendu, *Op. cit.* p. 19. "The Igbo world is based on an equalitarian principle. Equality or near equality ensures that no one person or group of persons acquires too much control over the life of others. This is an ideological obstacle to the development of a strong central authority. However, no human society achieves absolute equality among its citizens and Igbo society is no exception."

253 Uzukwu, *Op. cit.* p. 140.

254 The *Osu caste system* in Igboland is an issue that draws attention here, among others.

and would in concrete tackle some helplessness[255] and deficiencies; and so becomes an option for bringing out the best in all human beings, male and female. *A theological framework of this nature would not only be emancipatory but salvific and redemptive.*

This follows from the fact that a 'contextual theology' as this one here is also constantly a type of "ethics of liberation" – that is, an ethics of grace, liberation, and redemption of Igbo from their powerlessness and pathetic situation whereby they can become integrated as equals in the Nigerian church and society, and thus can find the path toward *meaning-full* life and action in the wider African society and in the World in general.

As much as this theological project is not an easy one in a complex culture like that of the Igbo; however an integral use of the metaphors and hermeneutics of the life-story in the gospel like that of the invitation of the vineyard owner to all the workers he met at various times to work in his vineyard (Mt 20:1–2), would help to exude from the lives of the Igbo any traces of obnoxious realities that are opposed to a real sense of being true witnesses 'together' – male and female, to the resurrection of Christ. Only then would they begin to realize the implication of the metaphorical statement of that 'Christ was not crucified in the church between two candles, but in the marketplace between two thieves' – a clarion call to witnessing concretely in the Igbo society in particular and Nigeria in general.

Indeed, the Igbo theology has an enormous task in this kind of complex situation. Creating the awareness is only a point on the line. The Igbo theologians, the hierarchy and entire laity joining hands to address these issues – to encourage 'co-responsible witnessing' in the Igbo church and society would be a bold step forward.

---

255 Uzukwu, *Ibid.* p. 2. "This image of apparent hopelessness, shared both by foreign friends and foes and by the daughters and sons of Africa, is disturbing. No continent or nation may survive or arise from the embers of such pessimism. Theology in Africa takes seriously this situation of misery and oppression as a context for its reflection. It does not adopt the simplistic approach of wishing our problems away, nor simply of denouncing the perpetrators of the evil. Rather, contextual theology in Africa tries to propose viable models for the reconstruction of our societies."

5.2 The Igbo Theology Vis-À-Vis The Church, Humanity, and World Order: The Challenge To Witnessing

The World Order is changing under our feet. No community is impervious. The Igbo theology in context being discussed here in this realm of the hermeneutics of witnessing cannot be ignore to these changes taking place under our feet, especially as these changes affect every facet of humanity and even the Church.

The issues of migration should be an issue of 'grave concern' to the Igbo society and local church[256] – as much as most of her people seem have migrated (internal – other parts of Nigeria or external – outside the Nigerian terrain) or are contemplating migration.

The 'Official Church' raises a concern on this issue, when John Paul II writes, "Religion opposes violence and raises up the hope of emigrants

---

256 The issue of migration is at the heart of concerns of most Western Countries today. There are times basic ambiguities that confront this issue – such as whether the persons are real refugees or economic miners or both. The clarification as to who is a refugee even becomes problematic as most Nation-States seem to depart from the Geneva Convention characterization (this definition is inclusive of, crossing border, well-founded fear, race, religion, nationality and membership of a social group) and even present day Roman Catholic characterization by the Pontifical Council for Migrants (victims of arms conflict, erroneous economic policies, natural disasters, internally displaced). Yet we discover that daily people who sought political asylum for example in Western Europe increases in Numbers. For the year 2001 the statistics registered almost 350, 000 people. We realize that there are reasons for most of these irregular migrants coming to Europe and the Americas, such as poverty – disparity between the rich and the poor, human right abuses, war, natural disasters. Some of these issues are human-made and some are beyond human control. But the former requires human efforts of control and solutions on the part of politicians, and not only them, but also equally engaging people's opinions not at the end but at the onset of making decisions on this matter. Concrete long-term reappraisal of Third World problems and the finding of authentic; lasting solutions are equally of great importance. The Igbo theology reflects on this from a perspective of Lazarus, the beggar in the story in the Scriptures vis-à-vis the Refugees story in the book of Exodus. Still God works in these types of situations today, or is He is not?

and refugees"[257]; added to this are the issues of globalization and cultural changes vis-à-vis politics, mass media today and the rest of us.

Mass media and the 'immaterial' means of communication: electronically transmitted codes (Internet) and images (television), these lead to time-space compression and to a dislocation of stable places, local habits, and forms of community life, in spite of the supposed lasting endurance of these forms. Advertising in view of consumption begins to fill the multilayered space of each one's life-world.[258] Hannerz gives the following striking illustration, "Switch on a television set in Kafachan a middle-sized, multi-ethnic, polyglot railroad junction (in Nigeria) at night, and you may see newscasts in English and Hausa, an old episode of *Charlie's Angels*, a concert by Hausa drummers, commercials for detergents, and bicycles, and a paid announcement of a funeral to take place in the nearest big city, where the TV station is located. The notion of funeral commercials struck me as an innovation at first, but obviously it is an extension of the concepts of full-page advertisements wealthy Nigerians take out in their daily newspapers to announce the burials of their loved ones."[259] This shows how much the media has affected the lives of people everywhere.

The media has not only affected the lives of the ordinary Igbo but has been a scapegoat in all sectors of the society. We see how much video, video game and television movies, local and foreign for the few who can afford them, are influencing lives of communities in Igboland – even to the detriment of those who cannot. It is arguably paradoxical that media has become "pervasive in their lives". Apart from thinking that this has become 'pervasive of their lives and privacies' one should also think that the good sides of the media should be appropriated to ennobling the spread of the faith – towards authentic witnessing, and enhancing the standard of living of the people.

---

257 *L'Osservatore Romano*, John Paul II in "True Religion opposes violence as offensive to the name of God" English Edition, n.22 (1745), 29th May2002, p. 4.
258 G. De Schrijver, *Contextual Theology. Developments in Third World Theologies of Liberation,* unpublished Lecture, Leuven, 1999–2000, p. 55.
259 U. Hannerz, *Cultural Complexity: Studies in the Social Organization of Meaning,* New York, 1992, p. 24.

Much of the impression the Western World has about the Igbo is based on images (and imaginations) the media, especially the foreign ones create. Furthermore, it is not out of place to see also the 'correlation' between the same media and the rest of the societal affairs in Igboland in particular and Nigeria in general in politics today. People who control the media industry in the country tend to use it only to their own advantages. Does this rather not call for authentic appropriation of the media to the good and promotion of the welfare of humans in Igbo society and enhancement of the faith among the people?

This thoughts are in line with Christina Holtz-Bacha of the Gutenberg University Mainz in *'the part the media play in today's political image making.'*[260] She recognized that politicians are dependent on the media in order to reach the wider public. It is worth seeing how politicians adapt themselves to the faces of the media in order to be known. In this way, we can see the 'correlation' between the media and politics. She reiterates that 'modernization' in which the Igbo are not left out, is the key term used to capture this change in social structure. With in this set up we notice – change of social structure, traditional social structures, social change, individualization, secularization, value change, dissolution of social structures pluralization of lifestyles and new structures.

This 'modernization' has led to the so-called neologism today, "lifestyle politics" which is not an easy term to define. An attempt at meaning on this neo-terminology is that in politics today, even in Igboland, the focus is on the 'lifestyle of the Politician', the role he or she performs and represents – in this sense, 'lifestyle has to do with the personalization of the Politician.' But this depends often on the fact that the politician has some media in favour of him or in the case of the church, if she has a media to back her interests and promote her aspirations.

'Lifestyle politics' is a reaction to changes in the society. Of which the wind blows rapidly across the globe even to the emerging Third World democracies. Political knowledge and awareness has been created courtesy of the media. In addition, Social capital, support for democracy and Political system, Political activism – sometimes fuelling affection and disaffection,

---

260 Politeia Conference, *Political Communication: The Rise of Lifestyle Politics and Its Consequences for Liberty*, Brussels, May 3rd, 2002.

cynicism, content and discontent among the Igbo especially with regard to how much the politicians are concerned about the people.

Here Igbo contextual theology being proposed comes into play not in the sense of providing an ethos for media and politics in Igboland today, but by way of encouraging a life of true witnessing in politics and governance on those who have been formed by the 'story of stories' – the resurrection of Christ. And in this way this theology can provide a hermeneutics of 'how' and 'what' it means to be truly human after the manner of Christ who gave himself – to caring and to be concerned in justice for humans, without the paradox of the 'logic of economic self-interest' among most Igbo politicians at the detriment of the people.[261]

---

261 L. Njoku, (Enugu, reporter), "Oputa, Ojukwu list way out of Igbo marginalisation" in *The Guardian*, Lagos, Friday, November 29, 2002. IKEMBA Nnewi, Chief Chukwuemeka Odumegwu Ojukwu and Human Rights Violations Investigation Commission's (HRVIC) Chairman, Justice Chukwudifu Oputa (rtd) yesterday called on *Ndigbo* to present a common front to enable them tackle the numerous problems facing them as a people. The duo spoke at the second edition of the yearly Igbo lecture series organised by the Enugu Sports Club in Enugu. According to Ojukwu, who was the chairman at the occasion, whereas the Igbo were of the views that the civil war fought over thirty years was over, and went into their homes to relax, other sections of the country still feel that the war must be fought from all fronts. He said: "Those who fought us know that the war has not ended. It is only *Ndigbo* that feels that the war has ended." He continued: "The problem of *Ndigbo* is that we don't know our enemies. Igbo should know that they don't have friends in Nigeria. We are not saying we should not stay in Nigeria. We should only know how to relate with them. If they say you don't know how to behave, know you are doing very well." Ojukwu, who elected to speak in Igbo at the occasion, therefore, asked the people to take over the mantle of leadership from him, adding that the battle he fought and all he did that had generated comments from within and outside the country was for the interest of Nigeria. He further renewed the call for an Igbo President, saying that an Igbo man has all the qualities to lead the country. He called on Nigerians to wake up to ask questions, especially on the antecedents of those who aspire to lead Nigeria, stressing that such was necessary because of the hostility that had always greeted certain office holders in the country. On his part, Justice Oputa, who delivered a keynote lecture titled: *Ndi-Igbo, Rediscovering ourselves*, told the gathering that *Ndigbo* would continue to make a vain claim of aspiring to leadership unless they come together like brothers and sisters? He lamented that while other sections of the country

This challenges to new ways of *theological conversation and witnessing* – that is embodying an alternative social vision for communities' vision and practices[262] in Igboland and to the 'global village', in this era of globalization, a-not-too-easy term to explain.

However, according to John Gray of the London School of Economics...In his discourse on *"Globalization after September 11"*[263]...his

---

could speak with one voice, the Igbo were always having divergent opinion on issues, pointing at the number of presidential aspirants emerging from Igbo land as an instance. "We can no longer speak together with one voice as a people. Imagine the number of presidential aspirants from Igboland. Unless we come together and harmonise our interest, our votes will be divided and we will lose out," he said. He added that the pursuit of personal interest has further taken away the truth from the people, stressing that in the olden days, *Ndigbo* were noted for transparency and hard work. Adding that *Ohanaeze Ndigbo* may not be a perfect organisation, he however, suggested that the people may join hands with the group for the needed reform to be achieved; stressing that a well-documented petition No.1648 brought by the *Ohanaeze* to the Human Rights Commission formed the basis of the discussion of the commission. "We need to put something in place and this will satisfy the yearnings of *Umuada Igbo*, this will show that we *Ndigbo* have succeeded in rediscovering ourselves," he counselled. In his speech, Enugu State Governor Chimaroke Nnamani lamented the unfortunate years spent in discussing a common front for *Ndigbo*. He suggested that in reality, what the Igbo needed was a discussion that could give room for debate and dialogue to provide the actual road for harmonisation of views. He stated that the challenge remained, among others, the realisation that the entire effort at making impact does not yield results when individual material accomplishment is allowed to impede the collective interest.

262 E. Katongole, *Op. cit.* p. 228.
263 Politeia Conference, *Loc. cit.* See also, J. Blanchard, *Where was God on September 11?* Darlington, 2002. "On 11 September 2001, terrorists hijacked four commercial airliners in the United States. Two were rammed into the twin towers of the World Trade Center in New York City and a third into the Pentagon in Washington, DC. Passengers on the fourth plane fought with the hijackers, but it crashed in Pennsylvania with the loss of all on board. In the most devastating terrorist attack in history, the world's tallest building had been reduced to rubble and some 3, 000 people blasted or crushed to death. The Times called it 'The day that changed the modern world'. Another newspaper claimed, 'History will never be the same again.' In a CNN Time Warner poll taken three months later, 73% of those interviewed said, 'it has changed everything for ever.'"(*Ibid.* Back-hardcover quote).

perspective, which was centered on his field of specialization as 'historian of ideas'...Two senses are distinguishable in this notion of globalization – whereby politicians talk of the type of economic requirement that came into being after the cold war – 'global free trade'. The risk that accompanies this is that it is worth noting that de-globalization took place in the 20th century. This is a result of the growth of nationalism after the world wars.

The second sense is the assumption that globalization and peace go together, whereas we have since after the world wars had other wars like the Gulf war and the Lwanda genocide. In this latter sense, globalization is connected with the new technology.

In connection with September 11, according to Gray, globalization witnessed the fact of State failure – in terms of communalized States against stronger States. Like in cases in history, globalization and State failure seem to go hand in hand. It is considered that States do have effects on economic growth, as was the case with the failure of the State of Russia. What happened, consequently on September 11 was a show of the weakness of a State – the fall of a weak State.

With September 11 people – seeing America's triumphalism and this made America vulnerable as since after the cold war. On the part of Europe, the impact is on the movement of peoples from zones of war to rich and stable Countries. The other side was the falling of the stagnant rich. In Europe the far right has exploited this against the opposition.

But the Igbo are not exempt from these influences. Of course we are all being 'globalized' – and being 'globalized' means much the same to all who 'are globalized'.[264]

Globalization is more durable as against – placed in reference to war and peace. However, if one thinks of globalization along the line of economic down turns, technology, one would surely emerge with some consequences. In this sense, what appears as 'globalization' for some, means localization for others; signaling a new freedom for some, upon many others it descends as an uninvited and cruel fate.[265]

---

264 Z. Bauman, *Globalization. The Human Consequences*, Oxford, 1998, p. 1.
265 "Globalisierung. Die Welt zerstoren oder gestalten (Dossier)," in *Publik-Forum. Zeitung Kritischer Christen*, no. 4, 22.February 2002, pp. 1–4. Among the issues

There is no doubt that the Igbo will be numbered in the latter cadre more than in the former. Mobility climbs to the rank of the uppermost among the coveted values – and the freedom to move, perpetually a scarce and unequally distributed commodity, fast becomes the main stratifying factor of our late-modern or postmodern times.[266]

One would notice that in this type of situation a new world order is in place though the earth and the heavens remain the same. The media and politico-economic ideologies vis-à-vis globalization are shifting these grounds under our feet with all their goodies and equally adverse effects. These mean a lot for the Igbo local churches and the wider society.

Globalization has its good sides – "through the increasing volume and rapidity of the flows of money, goods, people, information, technology, and images."[267] In spite of seeing on all angles the goodness of globalization one must not be blindfolded of the consequences globalization has on the lives of African countries in general.[268]

We know that a lot of sympathizers from some of the developed world brethren, by way of demonstrations and sometimes mutiny at locations where some of these globalization fora have been held, where the recent ones in Italy and Spain between the years, 2000–2002, have learnt us that behind the good sides of globalization there are equally misgivings about it on most humans.

And what is more, the free trade in which globalization swims is not afterwards so free! The rules are so thigh and have made exclusion of a lot of the brethren – who are also part and parcel of humanity and the World Order.

Yet we see the flexible approach of globalization, "A sports car is financed in Japan, drawn up in Italy and constructed in Indiana (USA),

---

raised within these pages are that, "Mehr arbeitslose und weniger demokratie", "Wenn China und Indien so leben wie wir", "Milliarden rasen um die Welt", "Die Reichen werden immer reicher", "Sozialstaat trotz globaler konkurrenz", "Faire Kleinkredite machen arme reicher".

266 Bauman, *Op. cit.* p. 2.
267 M. Featherstone, *Undoing Culture: Globalization, Postmodernity and Identity,* London, 1995, p. 81.
268 See, R. Braumann, *Afrika wird Totgefüttert. Plädoyer für eine neue Entwicklungspolitik,* Hamburg, Zurich, 1986.

in Mexico, and in France; it contains the most recent electronic components developed in New Jersey and constructed in Japan...Which of those products is a US one? Which one is not? How are we to decide? And is the answer really important?" And it is necessary too to add as much as work is provided with this diversification, but do the workers in the same level at the different places of 'localization' receive the same payment as much as some put in longer time?[269]

The complex issue of existential insecurity brought about by the process of globalization especially on the African countries' economies and general living standard need a first hand and eye-witness account, not that of some 'sensational media'. As Zygmunt Bauman writes, "the concerns with 'safety', more often than not trimmed down to the single-issue worry about the safety of the body and personal possessions, are 'overloaded', by being charged with anxieties generated by other, crucial dimensions of present-day existence – insecurity and uncertainty"[270] take their toll not only on the Igbo but on the entire humanity and World Order.

Igbo contextual theology in the light of the hermeneutics being articulated here will bring to bear a reassessing of the effects of the fore on humans and the need for envisioning the uniqueness of each people and what contribution their story can bring to bear on the growth of humanity; like the way Nnewi (in Igboland) local industries in South-east Nigeria are discovering their place in wider society of economic progress and self-reliance.

Nnewi (population 130, 000) which is located about 22 km South East of Onitsha in Anambra State, Nigeria, is a good example of an emerging alternative to the economic situation in which Nigeria like many other developing nations, finds itself as a result of global forces. As in most African countries south of the Sahara, this situation is characterized by the intervention of the IMF with its Structural Adjustment Programmes, the absence of foreign capital and the reluctance to invest in the Nigerian market for various reasons. Of course, this also showed how much the various governments of the Country have strangled the economy.

---

269 R. Reich, *L'économie mondialisée*, Paris, 1993, p. 103, quoted in F. Houtart, *The World-Encompassment of the Economy*, in CQ 68(1993–94) 2–10, p. 8.
270 Bauman, *Op. cit.* p. 5.

The effect of these and other factors has been a drawn-out economic depression. Nnewi is one of the examples where people have striven to find homegrown alternatives to the prevailing economic situation. A report of a workshop on "Alternative Development Strategies in Africa" organized by the Queen Elizabeth House in Oxford in 1989 and published in 1990 as part of Development Studies Working Papers makes a point of showing how Nigerian business people are striving to pull their country out of very difficult odds in the face of the global market-place. This report singles out Nnewi for particular mention.[271]

It notes that over the last decade the town of Nnewi has experienced relatively rapid industrialization. About 20 mediums to large-scale industries have been established across a variety of sectors. Since the end of the civil war in 1970, Nnewi locals have controlled some 80–90 per cent of the motor-parts trade in Nigeria. Nnewi's *Nkwo market* is the major import and wholesale point for motor spare parts in Nigeria.... The trade has proved a formidable generator of wealth and a major spur to industrialization (DSWP, 1990, p. 28).[272]

This industrialization of Nnewi is interesting because it is "entirely the product of private initiative and does not involve foreign investment" (DSWP, p. 29). Without the constraints which go with foreign capital and the selfishness and the short-sightedness of multinational corporations there is an attempt at Nnewi and other such centers around Nigeria to weather the negative effects of being pulled into a global market-place entirely on the conditions of other people. The industrialists of Nnewi are adapting foreign technology to local needs, providing employment to thousands and goods and services, which are relevant to the people's actual needs.[273]

On another note, the Igbo movies industry today is appropriating the worldview of their people to tell their own unique stories. The Igbo church and society are challenged in the light of the foregoing – to true witnessing from the richness of their people's worldview, cultural values and narrative toward self-reliance, a truly 'witnessing' church and progressive society.

---

271 P. I. Odozor, cssp. *Emerging African Alternatives to Globalization* (17 March 2002) in www.sedos.org/English/Odozor.htm consulted on 22 May 2002.
272 *Loc. cit.*
273 *Loc. cit.*

Chapter Six: Conclusion

The Igbo Contextual Theology for the Church and *Humans Integrally and Adequately Considered*[274]

One of the great problems in the past in doing theology, which is yet in vogue among most theologians today is to restrict and to think of theology in terms of mere intellectual enquiry without any *fundamentum in rei*, in the lives of peoples.[275] In this way, they "do not always have the best of reputations in matters of openness to human experience, to the world, to culture, to literature, to arts...Some of them may very well seem like bulls in china shops, attempting to proclaim certain dogmas in a univocal and merely descriptive language."[276] As good as this is in its own right and standing, but it falls inadequate, as much as one realizes the truism that, God is forever not removed from the plight and situation of His creation. Since the word "creation" itself indicates God's commitment. How then could God not be concerned with the promotion of human life and culture?[277]

The reason why some theologians do not think this way is that, "Often our "Christian" vision is too narrow, and we reduce the mission and reality of Christ to the level of what we have understood him to be. Rather than expanding "the Way, the Truth and the Life" as he who enlightens every human being coming into the world, and thus seeing the whole of history as the universal outreach of the Divine, the Divine reaching out to humanity, we have reduced the saving Reality to its historical expression in Jesus of Nazareth. Even though it has to be admitted that Christian faith says that in Jesus of Nazareth we have the perfect revelation of the Divine nature in God's relation to humanity,

---

274 This expression goes back to personalist, Professor Dr. Louis Jansen, outstanding Emeritus Professor of Moral Theology of the Catholic University Leuven, Belgium.
275 J. Haers, "A Risk Observed" in *Louvain Studies* 21(1996), pp. 46–59.
276 *Ibid.* p. 46.
277 *Ibid.* p. 47.

and that this Jesus of Nazareth is the incarnation of God's Reality, the saving Reality and its mission are not limited to the historical person Jesus."[278]

In this regard, the task facing theology, and indeed Igbo theology today is enormous, that of transposing theoretical beliefs into practical imperatives, so that the theological as such becomes a principle of action and hope for humanity becomes the end of theological investigations.[279]

In the light of Igbo contextual theology this would be achieved through reading meaning into the worldview of the Igbo and appropriating their values for witnessing via this 'story of stories' – the resurrection of Christ, as the 'hermeneutical metanarrative' of this theology.

Igbo worldview is shared by Christianity, added to this, is the belief that humankind is the custodian of the earth and not just its user. Since for the Igbo the past, present and the future generations form one community. The Igbo try to hold in tension the demands of the worldview of the elders and the necessity to build for the future – especially healthy human and community relations. A sense of wholeness of the person is manifested in the Igbo attitude to life and reality.

Just as there is no separation between the sacred and the secular in their communal life so to say, neither is there a separation between the soul and the body in a person.[280] In this way, the Igbo theology in context overcomes 'the Great fallacy' – "that the body was evil and the soul good, forsake earth for the sake of heaven, stamp out the flesh for the sake of blessedness."[281]

---

278 J. Kavunkal, "Ministry and Mission," in J. A. Scherer, & S. B. Bevan, *New Directions in Mission and Evangelization*, Vol. 2, New York, 1994, p. 92.
279 Dych, *Op. cit.*, p. 125; See also, *Ibid.* p. 143. Here, William V. Dych, a good commentator on Karl Rahner's Theology on the Eucharist was implying the Latter, on his implication of the transposing of Theology.
280 M. A. Oduyoye, "The Value of African Religious Beliefs and Practices for Christian Theology" in, *Op. cit.*, p. 112.
281 R. M. Brown, *Spirituality and Liberation*, Philadelphia, 1988, p. 27. It is worth noting "At two crucial points the church (sic) resisted this message. It rejected a view known as Docetism (from the Greek *dokeo*, meaning "to seem or appear to be"), which argued that Jesus only "seemed" to be human, since pure Deity could not dwell in impure flesh; and it also rejected a more

Since this fallacy which was in the past still persists today in different facets.[282]

The Igbo theology in context challenges to a commitment into the *Sitz im leben* of the people. One may ask, "What do the poor care for the niceties of a Nicaen or a Chalcedonian Christology, when survival itself is a luxury for them! What they need is the Jesus who actualized the concreteness and this-worldly dimension of the acceptable year of the Lord (Luke 4: 21), who can bring about this biblical Jubilee in their own immediate social and economic circles."[283]

Through the Igbo theology this people would articulate and express their faith in the most impressive way towards concrete witnessing in the One who witnessed to God and humanity through his Resurrection, Christ. Through this way, the Igbo theology in context contributes towards today's Church, humanity and World Order's well being.

Furthermore, as we saw in the case of the understanding of most 'sacrifices' – as a celebration in the Igbo context vis-à-vis the Christian Eucharist (the Sacramental Sacrifice[284]) which epitomizes the love of God in the death

---

complicated position known as Gnosticism, which held that salvation could come only from "inside" information or wisdom (gnosis) that was discovered by turning one's back on the world." *Loc. cit.*

282 *Ibid.* p. 31. "When Chilean bishops challenge General Pinochet for violations of human rights, he responds that they should be in the church praying. It is not only third world dictators who feel this way. Many conservative first world Christians likewise want religion to concentrate on "spiritual" things and stay away from challenges to political or economic injustice. To opt for "spirituality" means to them that things as they are need not be challenged, whereas to suggest that the love commandment means re-examining social structures that allow people to starve is, among other things, "unwarranted interference", a distortion of the gospel, a reduction to mere politics, a replacement of Jesus Christ by Karl Marx, a humanistic rather than a theocentric faith. The Catholic bishops' letter on the economy, for example, upsets many businessmen, because it suggests the need for changes in the capitalistic system of free enterprise. In sum, the appeal of the Great Fallacy is that it frees us from having to face challenges to the present state of affairs. It is a way of opting for the status quo."

283 J. Kavunkal, "Ministry and Mission," *Op. cit.* p. 94.

284 The Catechism of the Catholic Church, (Vatican City, 1992), Pauline Publications African, Kenya, 1995, p. 343. "We carry out this command of the Lord

and resurrection of Christ; its 'transpositioning,' as a 'reality' to be lived out, based on its proper understanding becomes a way of witnessing in today's world, of relating to other humans in love. This could be a most august type of spirituality for the Igbo and indeed for all humans today especially since after September 11.[285] And, this is au courant with the fact that, "the only way we encounter Jesus is through a thoroughly historical process. We arrive at our Christian identity through a process of socialization."[286]

In this way, the belief in one God who is love realized in the Eucharistic act becomes a source for one humanity. And thus renders all discrimination, racism and other types of ethnocentricity and exploitation of persons through political, economic, social and otherwise heretical and blasphemous.

Thus, with its worldview based on God, the Creator[287] – *Chineke*, the Igbo traditional beliefs; the Igbo Christianity may be in the vanguard of this movement for a better World Order,[288] of a united humanity of One God the Creator, the Father, and Provider of all for all and for the well being of all. This remains the most impressive and authentic way today for making the faith evergreen in Igboland, and nurturing Christians' spirituality across the globe for the 21st Century, in a world that has become a 'global village'.[289]

---

by celebrating the memorial of his sacrifice. In so doing, we offer to the Father what he has himself given us: the gifts of his creation, bread and wine which, by the power of the Holy Spirit and by the words of Christ, have become the body and blood of Christ. Christ is thus really and mysteriously made present."

285 See, J. Blanchard, *Where was God on September 11?* Darlington, 2002.
286 Richard, O.M.I, *Op. cit.*, p. 66.
287 M. A. Oduyoye, "The Value of African Religious Beliefs and Practices for Christian Theology", *Op. cit.* p. 111.
288 See, H. Kissenger, *World Order*, New York, 2014, p. 2. "Are we facing a period in which forces beyond the restraints of any order determine the future?" Cf. Amadi, E., *Ethics in Nigerian Culture*, Ibadan, 1982.
See also, F. Fukuyama, *Political Order and Political Decay: from the Industrial Revolution to the Globalisation of Democracy*, London, 2014, p. 4: "…weak government such as Mali, Niger, Nigeria, and Somalia. The reason that this part of the world is so much poorer in terms of income, health, education, and the like than booming regions like East Asia can be traced directly to the lack of strong government institutions."
289 G. Erlandson, (ed.), "Immigration and Its link to Interreligious Dialogue": Message of Pope John Paul II to Bishops' Conferences regarding the World

Since as it were, Christian faith is not merely about believing, professing and converting unbelievers and so called pagans, but more about witnessing in concrete from the background of the hermeneutics of the 'Christian metanarrative,' namely, as we said the Resurrection of Christ – the 'Story of Stories.' This is *au courant* with the fact that the Christian 'mission is to preserve the faith and bear witness to it with a life truly prophetic, so that the world may believe. This would be the Igbo way of showing that the 'Risen One is present.' And what is more, "let your witness, which cannot count on abundant resources, exercise its influence through the strength of Christ's grace, the leaven, which, though invisible, can make the whole loaf rise."[290]

Day for Migrants and Refugees (July, 25, 2001) in *The Pope Speaks*, Vol. 47, no. 3, p. 133. "In the course of these last decades, humanity has gradually taken on the features of a global village – where distances have become smaller and the network of communications more comprehensive."

290 John Paul II, "Your Mission is to Preserve the Faith and Bear Witness with Prophetic Life", in L'Osservatore Romano, 29th May 2002, pp. 5–6.

Bibliography

Achebe, C., *Things Fall Apart*, London, Ibadan, Nairobi, 1969.

Acholonu, C.O. Motherism. The Afrocentric Alternative to Feminism, Owerri, 1995.

Afigbo, A. E. (ed.), *Groundwork of Igbo History*, Lagos, 1992.

Agbasiere, J.T. *Women in Igbo Life and Thought*, London, 2000.

Ahiajoku Lecture, "Igbo World View and Contemporary living" published by Culture Division, Ministry of Information, Culture, Youth and Sports, 1984, Owerri.

Alberigo, G. Jossua, J-P & Komonchak, J. A. (eds.), transl. O'Connell, M.J. *The Reception of Vatican II*, Washington D.C., 1987.

Amadi, E., Ethics in Nigerian Culture, Ibadan, 1982.

Amadiume, I. *Male Daughters, Female Husbands*, Zed Books, 1987.

Appiah-kubi, K. & Torres, S. African Theology (papers from the Pan-African Conference of Third World Theologians, Dec 17–23, 1977, Accra, Ghana), New York, 1979.

Aquinas, T. *Summa Theologiae*, 111a.

Arinze, F.A. *Sacrifice in Ibo Religion*, Ibadan, 1970.

Arinze, F.A. *The Holy Eucharist*, Huntington, 2001.

Balasuriya, T. The Eucharist and Human liberation, London, 1979.

Basden, G. T. *Among the Ibos of Nigeria*, New York, 1982.

Bauman, Z. Globalization. The Human Consequences, Oxford, 1998.

Beckett, S. *Waiting for Godot. A Tragicomedy in Two Acts*, London, 2000, (first published 1956).

Bieringer, R. "Death and Resurrection of Christ. Effects on all" in Notes on Pauline interaction with the Corinthians, (part III, V), *Leuven Lecture notes*, Fifth year Master's programme, 2001.

Blanchard, J. Where was God On September 11? Darlington, Massachusetts, 2002.

Bloesch, D. G. Crumbling Foundations. Death & Rebirth In An Age of Upheaval, Michigan, 1984.

Boadt, L. & Smith, M. S. (eds.), *Imagery and Imagination: Biblical Essays in Honor of Aloysius Fitzgerald, F.S.C.* (The Catholic Biblical Quarterly Monograph, Series 32), Washington, 2000.

Boff, L. Jesus Christ Liberator. A Critical Christology for Our Time, New York, 1981.

Braumann, R. Afrika wird Totgefüttert. Plädoyer für eine neue Entwicklungspolitik, Hamburg, Zurich, 1986.

Brown, R. M. Spirituality and Liberation, Philadelphia, 1988.

Brueggemann, W. The Prophetic Imagination, (second edition), New York, 2001.

Bujo, B. "Can Morality be Christian in Africa?" in *African Christian Studies*, March 1988, Nairobi.

Candidus Of Fulda, "De Passione domini," 5; in J.P. MIGNE, *Patrologia Latina*, 106.68D-69A.

Carlyle, T. The French Revolution. A History, Volume I (The Bastille), Volume II (The Constitution,), Volume III (The Guillotine) London, 1837, (Reprinted. 2001, The Folio Society, London).

Congar, Y. "The Role of the Church in the Modern World" in H. Vorgrimler, (Eds.), et al. *Commentary on the Documents of Vatican II* (Vol. V). *Pastoral Constitution on the Church in the Modern World*, New York, 1969.

Congar, Y. "A Last look at the Council" in Stacpole, A. (ed), *Vatican II by Those Who Were There*, London, 1986.

Congar, Y. M-J. Jalons pour une théologie du laïcat, Unam Sanctam 23, Paris, 1953.

Crowder, M., The Story of Nigeria, London, 1962.

De Chardin, P. T. Le milieu divin essai de vie Intérieure, Paris, 1957.

De Schrijver, G. "Sacramentaliteits van Het Bestaan in de Overgang van Premoderniteit naar Moderniteit en PostModerniteit, in *J. Lamberts, Hedendaagse Accenten in de Sacramentologie*, Leuven, 1994.

D'costa, G. The Classic, Cambridge, 1983.

D'costa, G. (ed.), Christian Uniqueness Reconsidered: The Myth of a Pluralistic Theology of Religions, New York, 1990.

Die Deutschen Bischöfe, "Jesu Leben, sein Tod und seine Auferstehung als Anfang des wahren Friedens" in *Gerechter Friede*, no. 66, 27 September 2000, Bonn.

Dobson, T. How the Eucharist Can Transform Your Life, New York, 1993.

Education Department, United States Catholic Conference, *Faith and Culture*, Washington D.C., 1987.

Ehusani, G. O. An Afro-Christian Vision. "Ozovehe" Toward A More Humanised World, Lanham, New York, 1991, (reprinted 1997, Ibadan.).

Ehusani, G. O. A Prophetic Church, Ibadan, 1996.

Elnood, D.J. (ed.), *Asian Christian Theology: Emerging Themes*, Philadelphia, 1980.

Erlandson, G. (ed.), "Immigration and Its link to Interreligious Dialogue": Message of Pope John Paul II to Bishops' Conferences regarding the World Day for Migrants and Refugees in *The Pope Speaks*, Vol. 47, no. 3.

Farley, E. Divine Empathy: A Theology of God, Minneapolis, 1996.

Featherstone, M. Undoing Culture: Globalization, Postmodernity and Identity, London, 1995.

Fitzgerald, A. D. O.S.A.(ed), *Augustine Through the Ages: An Encyclopedia*, Michigan, Cambridge, 1999.

Fukuyama, F., Political Order and Political Decay: from the Industrial Revolution to the Globalisation of Democracy, London, 2014.

Gibellini, R. (ed.), *Paths of African Theology*, New York, 1994.

Girard, R. Le bouc émissaire, Paris, 1982.

Goldberg, M. Theology and Narrative: A critical Introduction, Nashville, 1982.

Gutierrez, G. Theology of Liberation, London, 1978.

Haers, J. "A Risk Observed" *Louvain Studies 21*(1996).

Hannerz, U. Cultural Complexity: Studies in the Social Organization of Meaning, New York, 1992.

Hauerwas, S. After Christendom, Nashville, 1991.

Hauerwas, S. The Peaceable Kingdom: A Primer in Christian Ethics, Notre Dame, 1983.

Hauerwas, S. A Community of Character: Toward a Constructive Christian Social Ethic, Notre Dame, 1981. Hauerwas, S. Truthfulness and Tragedy: Further Investigations in Christian Ethics, Notre Dame, 1977.

Hauerwas, S. After Christendom, Nashville, 1991.

Hick, J. And *Knittter, P.* (eds.), The Myth of Christian Uniqueness: Toward a Pluralistic Theology of Religions, New York, 1987.

Ijezie, L. E. (eds.), et al. Encounter. A Journal of African Life and Religion, Vol. 3, Rome, 1994.

Iroegbu, P. Kpim of Personality. Treatise on the Human person. Owerri, 2000.

Isichei, E. A History of the Igbo People, London, 1976.

John Paul II, "Christifideles laici," in *Origins.* 18, 1989.

Journals of the Rev. James Frederick Schoen and Mr. Samuel Crowther, London, 1842.

Katongole, E. Beyond Universal Reason. The Relation between Religion and Ethics in the Works of Stanley Hauerwas, Notre Dame, 2000.

Kavunkal, J. "Ministry and Mission," in J. A. Scherer, & S. B. Bevan, *New Directions in Mission and Evangelization,* Vol. 2, New York, 1994.

Kim, S. "God Reconciled His Enemy to Himself: The Origin of Paul's Concept of Reconciliation" in Longenecker, R. N. (edited), *The Road from Damascus. The Impact of Paul's Conversion on His life, Thought, and Ministry,* Michigan, Cambridge, 1997, pp. 102–122.

Kinoti, H.W., & Waliggo, J.M., (eds.), The Bible in African Christianity: Essays in Biblical Theology, Nairobi, 1997.

Kissinger, H., World Order, New York, 2014.

Koelber, J.F. Vatican II and Phenomenology. Reflections on the Life-World of the Church, Boston, 1985.

Kukah, M. H. Democracy and Civil Society in Nigeria, Ibadan, 1999.

Küng, H. (ed.), Yes To A Global Ethic, London, 1996.

Küng, H. "Global Politics and Global Ethic," *Unpublished Lecture*, Brussels, March 9, 2000.

Lane, D. "The Eucharist and Social Justice," in *The Eucharist and Unity*, Catholic Bishops" Conference of Nigeria, 1992.

Lanfranc Of Bec, "De corpore et sanguine Christi," in J.A. Giles (ed.), *Beati Lanfranci archiepiscopi Cantrarensis opera*, Vol. 2, Oxford, 1844.

Leijssen, L. "Current Theology. Sacramental Theology: A Review of Literature", *Theological Studies*, 55(1994), 661.

L'Osservatore Romano, (English edition), February 26, 1979.

MacHaffie, B.J. Her Story. Women In Christian Tradition, Philadelphia, 1986.

MacIntyre, A. Whose Justice? Which Rationality? Notre Dame, 1988.

MacIntyre, A. After Virtue. A Study in Moral Theory, (second edition), London, 1997.

Madiebo, A. The Nigerian Revolution and the Biafran War, Enugu, 1980.

Maloney, G.A. Mysticism and The new Age; Christic Consciousness in the new Creation, New York, 1991.

Martey, E. African Theology: Inculturation and Liberation, New York, 1993.

Mbiti, J.S., Bibel und Theologie im Afrikanischen Christentum, Göttingen, 1987.

Mbiti, J. "The Bible in African Culture," in Gibellini, R. (ed.), *Paths of African Theology*, New York, 1994.

Merrigan, T. & Haers, J. (eds.), The Myriad Christ. Plurality and the Quest for Unity in Contemporary Christology, Leuven, 2000.

Milbank, J. Theology and Social Theory, Cambridge, 1991.

Moltmann, J. Experiences in Theology. Ways and Forms of Christian Theology, M. KOHL (trans.), Minneapolis, 2000.

Mudge, L. S., "Hermeneutics" in A. Richardson & J. Bowden (eds.), *The Westminster Dictionary of Christian Theology*, Philadelphia, 1983.

Mueller-Vollmer, K. (ed.), *The Hermeneutics Reader*, New York, 1990.

Mueller D.L. Foundation of Karl Barth's Doctrine of Reconciliation, Jesus Christ Crucified and Risen (Toronto Studies in Theology, 54), 1991.

Ndiokwere, N. I., Prophecy and Revolution. The Role of Prophets in the Independent African Churches and in Biblical Tradition, London, 1981.

Newbigin, L. Truth and Authority in Modernity. (In the series, "Christian Mission and Modern Culture"), Pennsylvania, 1996.

New Jerusalem Bible (Standard Edition) London, 1985.

Nicolas, M-J. Théologie de la resurrection. Jesus la resurrection et la vie, Toulouse, 1982.

Nussbaum, M. The Fragility of Goodness, New York, 1986.

Nwosu, V. A. The Laity and The Growth of Catholic Church In Nigeria: The Onitsha Story 1903–1983, Onitsha, 1990.

Obi, C. A. (ed.), A Hundred Years of the Catholic Church in Eastern Nigeria 1885–1985, Onitsha, 1985.

Obilor, J.I., The Doctrine of the Resurrection of the Dead and the Igbo Belief in the "Reincarnation", Frankfurt am Main, Berlin, New York, 1993.

Odozor, P. I. Emerging African Alternatives to Globalization (17March, 2002), www.sedos.org/English/Odozor.htm, consulted on the 22 May 2002.

Ohadike, D.C. Anioma. A Social History of the Western Igbo People, Ohio, 1994.

Okere, T. African Philosophy. A Historico-Hermeneutical Investigation of the Conditions of its Possibility, New York, 1983.

Okuma, P. C. A Call to Authentic Living in Christ: The Challenge of the Third Millennium, Enugu, 1998.

Okuma, P.C. Towards an African Theology. The Igbo Context in Nigeria, Brussels, 2002.

Okure, T., & *Thiel, van P.,* (eds.). et. al. *Inculturation of Christianity in Africa,* Kenya, 1990.

Ozigboh, R. A. Igbo Catholicism: The Onitsha Connection 1967–1984, Onitsha, 1985.

Philips, G. The Role of the Laity in the Church, Gilbert, J. R. & Moudry, J. W. (trans.), Cork, 1955.

Politeia Conference, Political Communication: The Rise of Lifestyle Politics and Its Consequences for Liberty, Brussels, May 3rd, 2002.

Power, D. N. Sacrament: The Language of God's Giving, New York, 1999.

Publik-Forum, Zeitung Kritischer Christen, 25 January 2002.

Publik-Forum. Zeitung Kritischer Christen, no. 4, 22 February 2002.

Rahner, K. Theological Investigations. Man in the Church. Vol. II, K. H. Kruger (transl.), Baltimore, London, 1963.

Rahner, K. "Considerations on the Active Role of the Person in the Sacramental Event," in *Theological Investigations,* Vol. 14, Baltimore, Helicon, New York 1976.

Rahner, K. et al. (eds.), *Sacramantum Mundi. An Enclopaedia of Theology,* Vol. 2, Basle- Montreal, 1978.

Ratzinger, J. Kardinal, Salz der Erde. Ein Gesprach mit Peter Seewald, Stuttgart, 1998.

Reich, R. L'économie mondialisée, Paris, 1993, p. 103, quoted in F. Houtart, *The World-Encompassment of the Economy,* in CQ 68(1993–94) 2–10, p. 8.

Richard, L. O.M.I, et. al. (eds.), Vatican II. The Unfinished Agenda. A look to the Future, New York, 1987.

Ricoeur, P. Freud and Philosophy. An Essay on Interpretation, Connecticut, 1970.

Ricoeur, P. Hermeneutics and the human sciences, trans and edited by Thompson, J.B. New York, 1980.

Ricoeur, P. Soi-même comme un autre (l'ordre philosophique), Paris 1990.

Ricoeur, P. Time and Narrative (3 Volumes), *Mclaughlin, K. & Pellauer, D.* (translated), Chicago, 1984–1988.

Rossi, P. (ed.), et al. Philosophy and Theology. Marquette University Journal, Vol. 11, no. 1(1998).

Scherer, J. A. & Bevans, S.B. (eds.) Vol. 2, New York, 1994. *New Directions in Mission & Evangelization. Theological Foundations,* New York, 1994.

Schillebeeckx, E. Christ: The Experience of Jesus As Lord, Bowden, J. (translated), New York, 1989.

Schineller, P. A Handbook on Inculturation, New York, 1990.

Schwöbel, C. (Conference paper), God as Conversation. Reflections on a Theological Ontology of Communicative Relations, Leuven, November 7, 2001.

Smith, S. G. "Three Religious Attitudes" in P. Rossi, (eds.), *Philosophy and Theology,* Marquette University Journal, Vol. 11, No. 1, 3.

Sobrino, J. The Principle of Mercy: Taking the Crucified People from the Cross, New York, 1984.

Tanner, N. P. S.J. (ed.) Decrees of the Ecumenical Councils, Vol. II (Trent to Vatican II), London, 1990.

The Catechism Of The Catholic Church, English translation, Kenya, 1995.

The Guardian, Lagos, Friday, November 29, 2002.

The Mother of the Redeemer, U.S.A., Catholic Conference, No. 44.

Thomasset, A. Poétique de l'existence et agir moral en société. La contribution de Paul Ricoeur au fondement d'une éthique herméneutique et narrative, dans une perspective chrétienne, Louvain, 1995.

Tillich, P. Dynamics of Faith, New York, 1957.

World Council of Churches, *Towards an Ethic of Global Responsibility*, Chicago, U.S.A. 4 September 1993.

Uchendu, V.C. The Igbo of Southeast Nigeria, Forth Worth, Philadelphia, London, Tokyo, 1965.

Ukpong, J.S. "Christology and Inculturation: A New Testament Perspective" in *Gibellini, R.* (ed.), *Paths of African Theology*, New York, 1994, pp. 40–61.

Urs von Balthasar, H. Mysterium Paschale: The Mystery of Easter, Nichols, A. (translated), Michigan, 1990.

Uzukwu, E. E., A Listening Church: Autonomy and Communication in African churches, New York, 1996.

Verstraeten, J. "The 'World' of the Bible as Meta-Ethical Framework of Meaning for Ethics: An Interpretation," in *Vroom, H. M. & Gort, J. D.*, (eds.), Holy *Scriptures in Judaism, Christianity and Islam. Hermeneutics, Values and Society*, Amsterdam/Atlanta, 1997.

Verstraeten, J. (trans.), The Rediscovery of Meaning in Professional life: Perspectives for Spirituality of the Laity in the Twenty-first Century, Leuven, 1999.

Verstraeten, J. Beyond Business Ethics: Leadership, Spirituality and the Quest for Meaning, Leuven, 2000.

Wittgenstein, L. Philosophical Investigations. Anscombe, E. (trans.), New York, 1953.

3RD International Lest Congress of Leuven *Encounters in Systematic Theology*, November 6–9, 2001.

About The Book

One of the great problems in the past in doing theology, which is still very much in vogue (whereas should not be today in light of today's challenges) among most theologians and 'thologies' today is to restrict and to think of 'theology' only in terms of *mere intellectual enquiry* without any *fundamentum in rei* – in the concrete lives of peoples. This Book, *The Hermeneutics of African-Igbo Theology* is aimed at overcoming this gap. It establishes this reality through the "story of all stories" – the Resurrection of Christ as the foundation and hermeneutics of/for doing theology in concrete *qua tale;* especially as it affects Africans (the Igbo).

This book should be read alone on its own and seen on its face as such or as the case might be seen as a follow up 'volume 2' to my earlier book *(Towards an African Theology: The Igbo Context in Nigeria*, Peter Lang Academic Publishers, Frankfurt am Main, New York, Berlin, Wein, 2002 – under the academic title series: *Gods, Humans and Religions,* edited by Prof. Dr. Gabriel Frágniére – Former Rector of the College of Europe (Bruges) and Professor of the Central European University (Warsaw).

Peter Chidi Okuma is a priest of the diocese of Orlu, Nigeria. He holds a Diploma with Distinction in Freelance and Feature Writing in Journalism from The London School of Journalism, United Kingdom. He also holds three Masters degrees in Religious Studies, Education/Psychology, and Theology from the Catholic University of Leuven, Belgium, where he obtained a certified doctoral training in Theology in 2005, and proceeded to obtain a doctorate in Theology at the Ludwig Maximillian University Munich Germany and a second doctorate in Social Science at St. Thomas Aquinas University Rome (Angelicum). He has authored many national and International books and articles. He currently resides and works in Germany.

Other Books by Peter Chidi Okuma published by Peter Lang Academic Publishers:

1. TOWARDS AN AFRICAN THEOLOGY. THE IGBO CONTEXT IN NIGERIA, Peter Lang Publishers, Bruxelles, Frankfurt, Bern, New York, Oxford, 2002.

2. OMUMU – THE IGBO LIFE-VALUE: A CHALLENGE TO HUMAN LIFE ISSUE TODAY (with Particular Focus on *Humanae Vitae* In light of Familial value study) – An Analytical-Practical Approach, Peter Lang Publishers, Frankfurt am Main, New York, 2008.

3. EMPOWERMENT OF THE CATHOLIC LAITY IN THE NIGERIAN POLITICAL SITUATION. A Hermeneutical Reading of *Apostolicam Actuositatem* (the decree on the Apostolate of the Laity of Vatican II and it's application to concrete situation, Peter Lang Academic Publishers, Frankfurt am Main, New York, 2008.

4. THE VATICAN II: THE LAITY AND TODAY'S CHALLENGES, Peter Lang Academic Publishers, Frankfurt am Main, New York, 2011.

5. *Beyond Witnessing: A New Way of Humanizing the World*, Peter Lang Academic Publishers, Frankfurt am Main, New York, 2013.

www.ingramcontent.com/pod-product-compliance
Ingram Content Group UK Ltd.
Pitfield, Milton Keynes, MK11 3LW, UK
UKHW041922210426
5322IPUK00002B/3